MW01532797

THIS BOOK BELONGS TO

_____

START DATE

_____

SHE READS TRUTH

FOUNDERS

FOUNDER
Raechel Myers

CO-FOUNDER
Amanda Bible Williams

EXECUTIVE

CHIEF EXECUTIVE OFFICER
Ryan Myers

EDITORIAL

MANAGING EDITOR
Lindsey Jacobi, MDiv

PRODUCTION EDITOR
Hannah Little, MTS

ASSOCIATE EDITOR
Kayla De La Torre, MAT

COPY EDITOR
Becca Owens, MA

CREATIVE

SENIOR ART DIRECTOR
Annie Glover

DESIGN MANAGER
Kelsea Allen

DESIGNERS
Savannah Ault
Ashley Phillips

MARKETING

MARKETING LEAD
Kelsey Chapman

PRODUCT MARKETING MANAGER
Krista Squibb

CONTENT MARKETING STRATEGIST
Tameshia Williams, ThM

SOCIAL MEDIA SPECIALIST
Bella Ponce

OPERATIONS

OPERATIONS DIRECTOR
Allison Sutton

COMMUNITY ENGAGEMENT

COMMUNITY ENGAGEMENT MANAGER
Delaney Coleman

COMMUNITY ENGAGEMENT SPECIALISTS
Cait Baggerman
Katy McKnight

SHIPPING

SHIPPING MANAGER
Marian Welch

FULFILLMENT LEAD
Hannah Song

FULFILLMENT SPECIALISTS
Bonnie Nickander
Kelsey Simpson

SUBSCRIPTION INQUIRIES
orders@shereadstruth.com

SHE READS TRUTH™

© 2025 by She Reads Truth, LLC
All rights reserved.

All photography used by permission.

ISBN 978-1-962221-38-2

1 2 3 4 5 6 7 8 9 10

No part of this publication may be reproduced, distributed, or transmitted in any form or by any means, including photocopying, recording, or other electronic or mechanical methods, without the prior written permission of She Reads Truth, LLC, except in the case of brief quotations embodied in critical reviews and certain other noncommercial uses permitted by copyright law.

All Scripture is taken from the Christian Standard Bible®, Copyright © 2020 by Holman Bible Publishers. Used by permission. Christian Standard Bible® and CSB® are federally registered trademarks of Holman Bible Publishers.

Though the dates, locations, and individuals in this book have been carefully researched, scholars disagree on many of these topics.

Research support provided by Logos Bible Software™. Learn more at logos.com.

@SHEREADSTRUTH

Download the She Reads Truth app, available for iOS and Android

Subscribe to the She Reads Truth Podcast

SHEREADSTRUTH.COM

This book was printed offset in Nashville, Tennessee, on 70# Lynx Opaque. Cover is 100# Cougar Opaque with a soft touch lamination.

NEHEMIAH
REBUILD AND RENEW

SHE READS TRUTH

IN THE MIDDLE OF THE
VERY REAL OPPOSITION AND
INJUSTICE IN THIS STORY,
THERE IS A GOD OF GREAT
PATIENCE, COMFORT, AND HOPE.

Kayla

Kayla De La Torre
ASSOCIATE EDITOR

A few winters ago, the pipes burst in my in-laws' home while they were out of town. My husband and I drove over to take photos and give them an idea of how bad the damage was. As we tentatively opened the front door, we pushed aside soggy clumps of insulation, chunks of dry wall, and even decor that had been flung by the rushing water. To say that their home was destroyed would be an understatement (fun fact: ceilings are NOT supposed to be on the floor). At one point in our very careful survey of the wreckage, we simply paused to take in the scene. Wet furniture was already molding. Paint bubbled and peeled off the walls. Pieces of debris littered the ground. This once warm, welcoming, and lovely home was absolutely destroyed. And standing in those chaotic remains, I had no idea how to even begin restoring all that was lost.

I imagine Nehemiah having a similar experience on his night ride around the demolished walls of Jerusalem (you'll get a visual of that route in "The Walls of Jerusalem in Nehemiah's Time" on page 50). What had once been the home of God's people—a place where they interacted with neighbors, shared meals, and simply lived out regular days—was now an unprotected pile of rubble. How was Nehemiah going to take this broken place and make it the haven that it once was?

Thankfully, Nehemiah wasn't the one who had to answer that question—the book of Nehemiah tells us exactly how God rebuilt both the walls of Jerusalem and the spiritual identity of His people. In the middle of the very real opposition and injustice in this story, there is a God of great patience, comfort, and hope. The Lord strengthened His people for the work they needed to do in order to restore their physical home. When they failed to live up to their spiritual calling as His chosen nation, God did not abandon them and instead called them back to His law and its wisdom. God upheld His covenant promise to be faithful to them even when they could not do the same in return.

As we read the book of Nehemiah, we will dig deep to see how the struggles and experiences of God's people resonate in our own lives. We will turn our hearts to the God of Nehemiah, the same God who steadfastly restores us when we repent from sin and return to Him. And we will give thanks to the Lord that, in Christ, He has provided all we need to find our sure, safe, and unshakeable home in Him.

Design *on* Purpose

At She Reads Truth, we believe in pairing the inherently beautiful Word of God with the aesthetic beauty it deserves. Each of our resources is thoughtfully and artfully designed to highlight the beauty, goodness, and truth of Scripture in a way that reflects the themes of each curated reading plan.

Because the book of Nehemiah tells the story of God restoring His people both physically and spiritually, we wanted to visualize this rebuilding with the landscapes, textures, and shapes of rubble. Rocks embody the strength and resilience that rebuilding requires, but at the same time, they don't always fit perfectly together. Like the working conditions under which God's people labored and the spiritual condition of their hearts, the formation of rocky landscapes is not a clean or straightforward process. The dust of broken rocks reminds us to trust in the same God who formed humanity from dust as the only hope for true restoration.

HOW TO USE THIS BOOK

She Reads Truth is a community of women dedicated to reading the Word of God every day. In this **Nehemiah** reading plan, we will read the book of Nehemiah, along with complementary passages of Scripture, to see how God restored His holy city and people.

READ & REFLECT

Your **Nehemiah** book focuses primarily on Scripture, with added features to come alongside your time with God's Word.

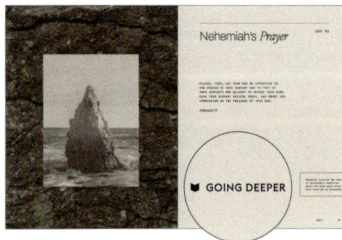

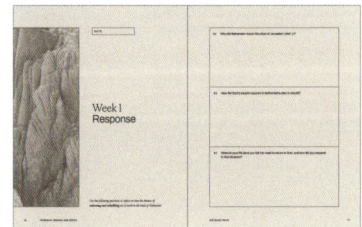

SCRIPTURE READING

Designed for a Monday start, this three-week reading plan presents the book of Nehemiah in daily readings, along with additional passages curated to show how the theme of the main reading can be found throughout Scripture.

🐦 *Additional passages are marked in your daily reading with the Going Deeper heading.*

RESPONSE

Each week features questions for reflection.

COMMUNITY & CONVERSATION

You can start reading this book at any time! If you want to join women from Nolensville to Northern Ireland as they read along with you, join us in the **Nehemiah** reading plan through our app or website and podcast.

SHE READS TRUTH APP

Devotionals corresponding to each daily reading can be found in the **Nehemiah** reading plan in the She Reads Truth app. You can use the app to participate in community discussion and more.

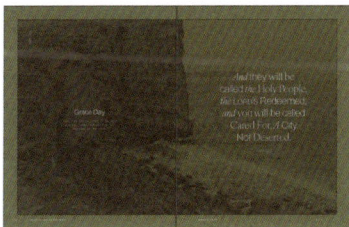

GRACE DAY

Use Saturdays to catch up on your reading, pray, and rest in the presence of the Lord.

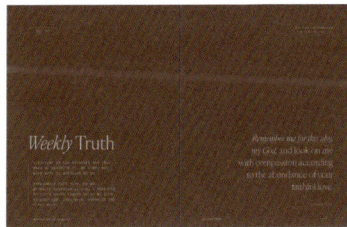

WEEKLY TRUTH

Sundays are set aside for Scripture memorization.

See tips for memorizing Scripture on page 100.

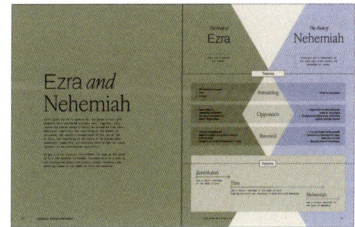

EXTRAS

This book features additional tools to help you gain a deeper understanding of the text.

Find a complete list of extras on page 11.

SHEREADSTRUTH.COM

The **Nehemiah** reading plan and devotionals will also be available at SheReadsTruth.com as the community reads each day. Invite your family, friends, and neighbors to read along with you!

SHE READS TRUTH PODCAST

Subscribe to the She Reads Truth Podcast, and join our founders and their guests each week as they talk about what you'll read in the week ahead.

Tune into episodes 295–297 for our **Nehemiah** *series.*

Table *of* Contents

Week One

Week Two

Week Three

So I said to them, "You see the trouble we are in. Jerusalem lies in ruins *and* its gates have been burned. Come, let's rebuild Jerusalem's wall, so that we will no longer be *a* disgrace."

Nehemiah 2:17

She Reads Nehemiah

Though appearing earlier in the Protestant Bible, chronologically Nehemiah is one of the final books of the Hebrew Bible. Nehemiah's ministry in Jerusalem occurred in 444 BC, and the book of Nehemiah was written soon after in the late fifth century BC.

While most of the nation lived in exile in Babylon after the temple in Jerusalem was destroyed in 586 BC, the Hebrew people were released in 538 BC by a decree of King Cyrus of Persia that allowed them to return to Jerusalem. Over time, they returned in three main groups: the first led by Zerubbabel (the governor of Judah), the second led by Ezra (a prominent priest and scribe), and the third led by Nehemiah.

Nehemiah was the cupbearer to the Persian king Artaxerxes I. He returned to Jerusalem under a special leave of absence from the king, was appointed governor of Judah (5:14), and led those who had already returned in rebuilding the walls, resettling Jerusalem, and reestablishing the law in Israel.

The book of Nehemiah is written from the perspective of Nehemiah, though the author is never specifically named. The books of Ezra and Nehemiah were regarded as a single text until they were split into two separate works around the third century AD. Because Ezra is called a scribe in both Ezra and Nehemiah, the oldest Jewish sources usually credit Ezra as the author of both texts.

The book of Nehemiah records the rebuilding of the walls in Jerusalem despite external opposition and internal difficulties in reestablishing God's law. Nehemiah repeatedly sought God's favor, forgiveness, and remembrance for himself and for the nation as they navigated the perils of the postexilic world. Yet despite these efforts, the books of Ezra and Nehemiah both record the continued disobedience of the people as they failed to keep their own covenant commitments.

Here are few key themes to look for as you read:

1 Returning and Rebuilding

Nehemiah exhorted the people to remain faithful to the Lord and return to Him, leading both the physical and spiritual restoration of God's people.

2 Endurance Through Opposition

Though challenges arose from all sides, God's people endured because of His strength and protection over them.

3 Repentance and Renewal

Though they imperfectly followed God's law, the nation of Israel turned back to its commands to restore their purpose and identity as God's holy people.

The events of the books of Nehemiah—the rebuilding of the walls, the stabilizing of Jerusalem, and the development of a communal identity for the nation—all reveal how the heart of God is set on the rescue and restoration of His beloved creation. Great strength and resiliency are found in God's power as His people endured their trials and fears with His presence as their guard. Nehemiah's devoted obedience to the Lord is an example to us as we follow God's purpose in our lives.

Nehemiah's *Prayer*

PLEASE, LORD, LET YOUR EAR BE ATTENTIVE TO
THE PRAYER OF YOUR SERVANT AND TO THAT OF
YOUR SERVANTS WHO DELIGHT TO REVERE YOUR NAME.
GIVE YOUR SERVANT SUCCESS TODAY, AND GRANT HIM
COMPASSION IN THE PRESENCE OF THIS MAN.

Nehemiah 1:11

Nehemiah 1

[1] The words of Nehemiah son of Hacaliah:

NEWS FROM JERUSALEM

During the month of Chislev in the twentieth year, when I was in the fortress city of Susa, [2] Hanani, one of my brothers, arrived with men from Judah, and I questioned them about Jerusalem and the Jewish remnant that had survived the exile. [3] They said to me, "The remnant in the province, who survived the exile, are in great trouble and disgrace. Jerusalem's wall has been broken down, and its gates have been burned."

> Nehemiah received the news of Jerusalem's condition about thirteen years after Ezra returned to Jerusalem.

NEHEMIAH'S PRAYER

⁴ When I heard these words, I sat down and wept. I mourned for a number of days, fasting and praying before the God of the heavens. ⁵ I said,

Lᴏʀᴅ, the God of the heavens, the great and awe-inspiring God who keeps his gracious covenant with those who love him and keep his commands, ⁶ let your eyes be open and your ears be attentive to hear your servant's prayer that I now pray to you day and night for your servants, the Israelites. I confess the sins we have committed against you. Both I and my father's family have sinned. ⁷ We have acted corruptly toward you and have not kept the commands, statutes, and ordinances you gave your servant Moses. ⁸ Please remember what you commanded your servant Moses: "If you are unfaithful, I will scatter you among the peoples. ⁹ But if you return to me and carefully observe my commands, even though your exiles were banished to the farthest horizon, I will gather them from there and bring them to the place where I chose to have my name dwell." ¹⁰ They are your servants and your people. You redeemed them by your great power and strong hand. ¹¹ Please, Lord, let your ear be attentive to the prayer of your servant and to that of your servants who delight to revere your name. Give your servant success today, and grant him compassion in the presence of this man.

At the time, I was the king's cupbearer.

◣ GOING DEEPER

Psalm 137

LAMENT OF THE EXILES

¹ By the rivers of Babylon—
there we sat down and wept
when we remembered Zion.
² There we hung up our lyres
on the poplar trees,
³ for our captors there asked us for songs,
and our tormentors, for rejoicing:
"Sing us one of the songs of Zion."

⁴ How can we sing the Lᴏʀᴅ's song
on foreign soil?
⁵ If I forget you, Jerusalem,
may my right hand forget its skill.
⁶ May my tongue stick to the roof of my mouth
if I do not remember you,
if I do not exalt Jerusalem as my greatest joy!

[7] Remember, LORD, what the Edomites said
that day at Jerusalem:
"Destroy it! Destroy it
down to its foundations!"
[8] Daughter Babylon, doomed to destruction,
happy is the one who pays you back
what you have done to us.
[9] Happy is he who takes your little ones
and dashes them against the rocks.

Matthew 23:37–39

JESUS'S LAMENTING OVER JERUSALEM

[37] "Jerusalem, Jerusalem, who kills the prophets and stones those who are sent to her. How often I wanted to gather your children together, as a hen gathers her chicks under her wings, but you were not willing! [38] See, your house is left to you desolate. [39] For I tell you, you will not see me again until you say, 'Blessed is he who comes in the name of the Lord'!"

Nehemiah Sent *to* Jerusalem

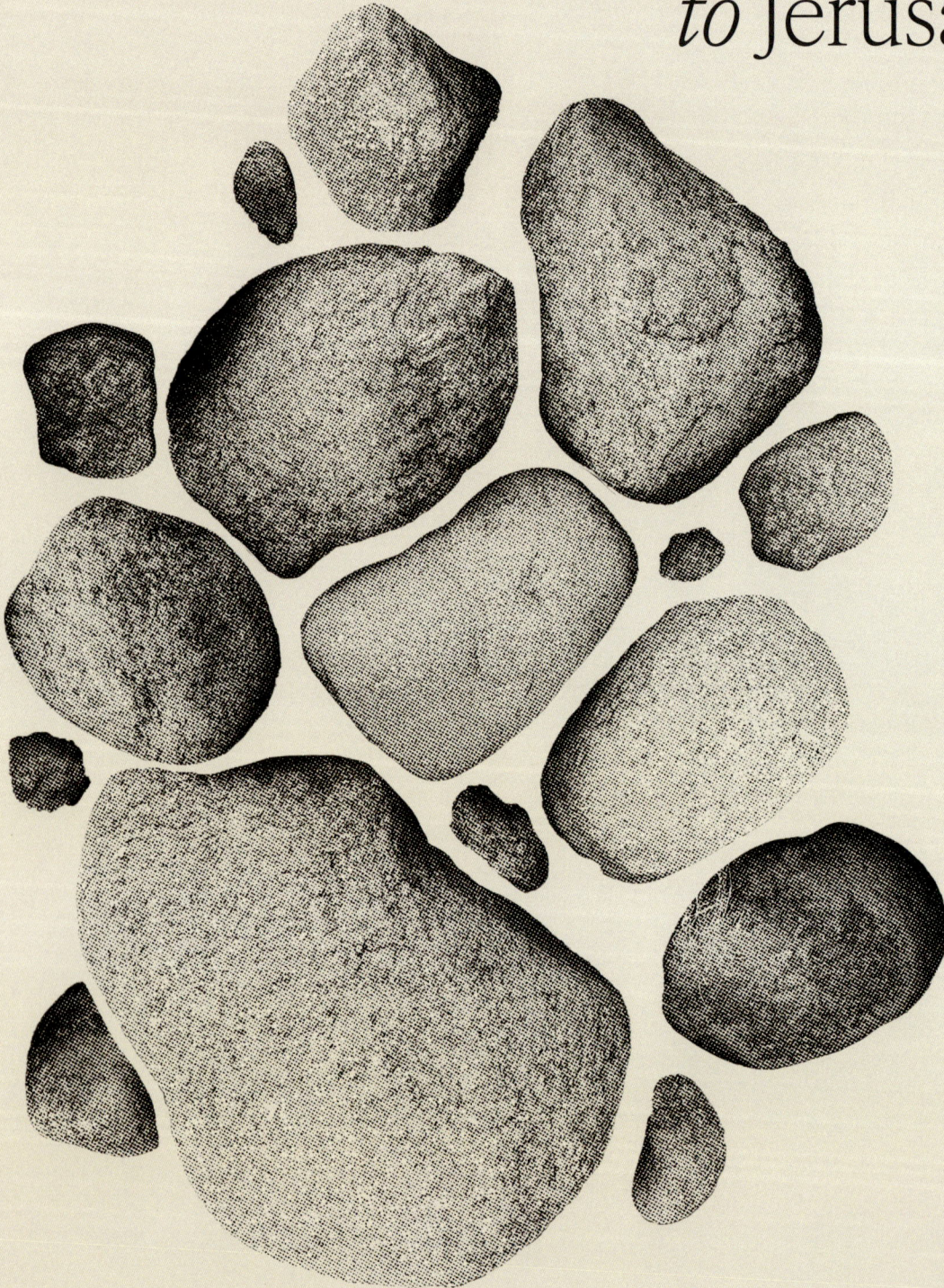

Nehemiah 2:1–10

NEHEMIAH SENT TO JERUSALEM

[1] During the month of Nisan in the twentieth year of King Artaxerxes, when wine was set before him, I took the wine and gave it to the king. I had never been sad in his presence, [2] so the king said to me, "Why do you look so sad, when you aren't sick? This is nothing but sadness of heart."

I was overwhelmed with fear [3] and replied to the king, "May the king live forever! Why should I not be sad when the city where my ancestors are buried lies in ruins and its gates have been destroyed by fire?"

[4] Then the king asked me, "What is your request?"

So I prayed to the God of the heavens [5] and answered the king, "If it pleases the king, and if your servant has found favor with you, send me to Judah and to the city where my ancestors are buried, so that I may rebuild it."

[6] The king, with the queen seated beside him, asked me, "How long will your journey take, and when will you return?" So I gave him a definite time, and it pleased the king to send me.

[7] I also said to the king, "If it pleases the king, let me have letters written to the governors of the region west of the Euphrates River, so that they will grant me safe passage until I reach Judah. [8] And let me have a letter written to Asaph, keeper of the king's forest, so that he will give me timber to rebuild the gates of the temple's fortress, the city wall, and the home where I will live." The king granted my requests, for the gracious hand of my God was on me.

[9] I went to the governors of the region west of the Euphrates and gave them the king's letters. The king had also sent officers of the infantry and cavalry with me. [10] When Sanballat the Horonite and Tobiah the Ammonite official heard that someone had come to pursue the prosperity of the Israelites, they were greatly displeased.

King Artaxerxes I was the ruler of the Persian Empire from 464–424 BC. He was the son of Ahasuerus (also known as Xerxes), who was the king of Persia during the time of Esther.

◆ GOING DEEPER

Deuteronomy 30:1–6

RETURNING TO THE LORD

[1] When all these things happen to you—the blessings and curses I have set before you—and you come to your senses while you are in all the nations where the LORD your God has driven you, [2] and you and your children return to the LORD your God and obey him with all your heart and all your soul by doing everything I am commanding you today, [3] then he will restore your fortunes, have compassion

on you, and gather you again from all the peoples where the Lord your God has scattered you. [4] Even if your exiles are at the farthest horizon, he will gather you and bring you back from there. [5] The Lord your God will bring you into the land your ancestors possessed, and you will take possession of it. He will cause you to prosper and multiply you more than he did your ancestors. [6] The Lord your God will circumcise your heart and the hearts of your descendants, and you will love him with all your heart and all your soul so that you will live.

Amos 9:11–15

ANNOUNCEMENT OF RESTORATION

[11] In that day
I will restore the fallen shelter of David:
I will repair its gaps,
restore its ruins,
and rebuild it as in the days of old,
[12] so that they may possess
the remnant of Edom
and all the nations
that bear my name—
    this is the declaration of the Lord; he will do this.

[13] Look, the days are coming—
    this is the Lord's declaration—
when the plowman will overtake the reaper
and the one who treads grapes,
the sower of seed.
The mountains will drip with sweet wine,
and all the hills will flow with it.
[14] I will restore the fortunes of my people Israel.
They will rebuild and occupy ruined cities,
plant vineyards and drink their wine,
make gardens and eat their produce.
[15] I will plant them on their land,
and they will never again be uprooted
from the land I have given them.
The Lord your God has spoken.

Day 2
Notes

Nehemiah *in* Postexilic History

As prophesied by Jeremiah, the people of Judah lived in exile for seventy years. God was faithful to restore His people to the land He had given them. After the completion of the seventy years under Babylonian rule, groups began to return and rebuild both the temple of God and the city of Jerusalem.

The following page includes a timeline with key dates showing how Nehemiah fits into the period of history following the exile. Also highlighted are key moments concerning the temple and walls of Jerusalem and the three main groups of exiles who returned to Jerusalem.

King Cyrus of Persia issues a decree allowing exiles from Judah to return to the promised land and rebuild the temple.

Led by Zerubbabel, a group of exiles return from Persia to the promised land.

The second temple is completed in Jerusalem under the leadership of Zerubbabel and the prophets Haggai and Zechariah.

The returned exiles dedicate the temple and celebrate Passover.

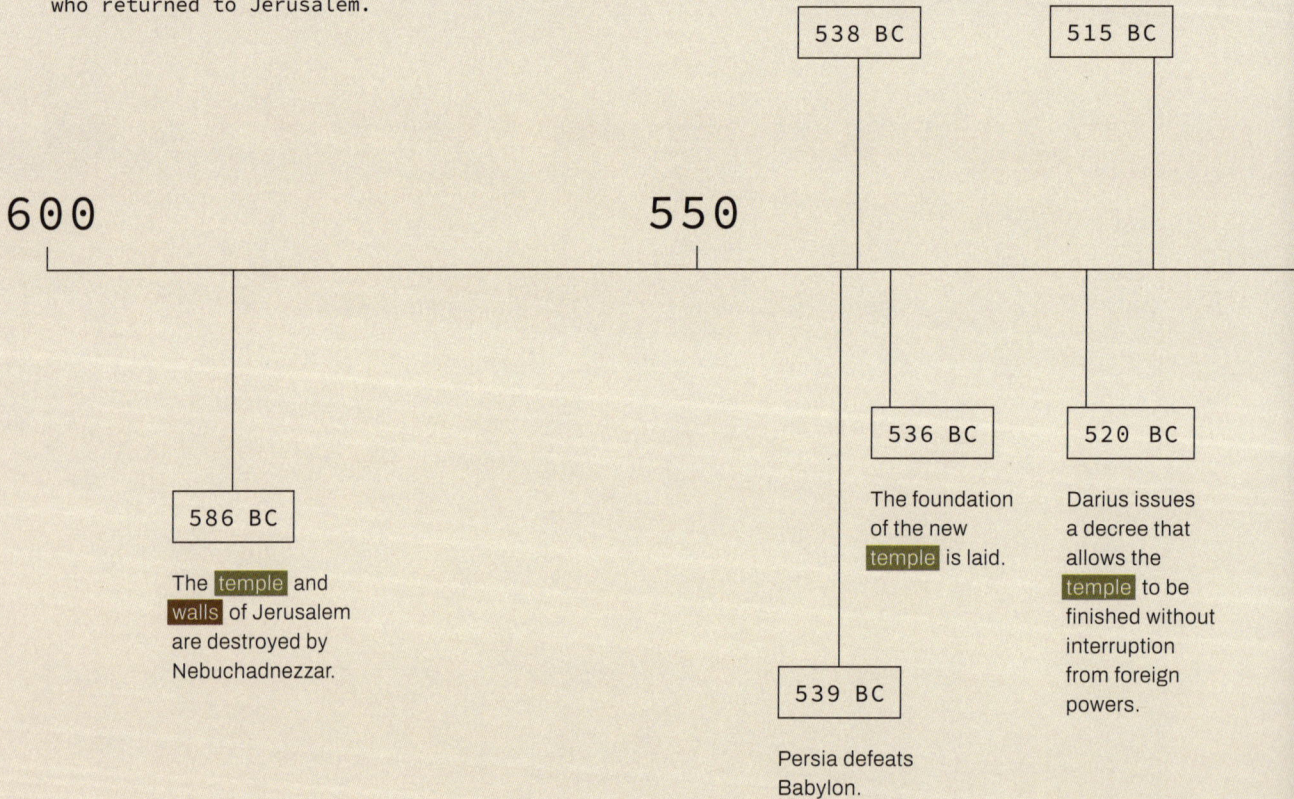

538 BC

515 BC

600

550

586 BC

The temple and walls of Jerusalem are destroyed by Nebuchadnezzar.

536 BC

The foundation of the new temple is laid.

520 BC

Darius issues a decree that allows the temple to be finished without interruption from foreign powers.

539 BC

Persia defeats Babylon.

Esther intercedes with King Ahasuerus on behalf of her people still living in Persia.

While serving in the Persian city of Susa, Nehemiah learns that Jerusalem is still in great disrepair.

Led by Nehemiah, a group of exiles return from Persia to the promised land to rebuild the walls of Jerusalem.

KEY

474 BC

Ezra reestablishes worship in Jerusalem.

444 BC

457 BC

450

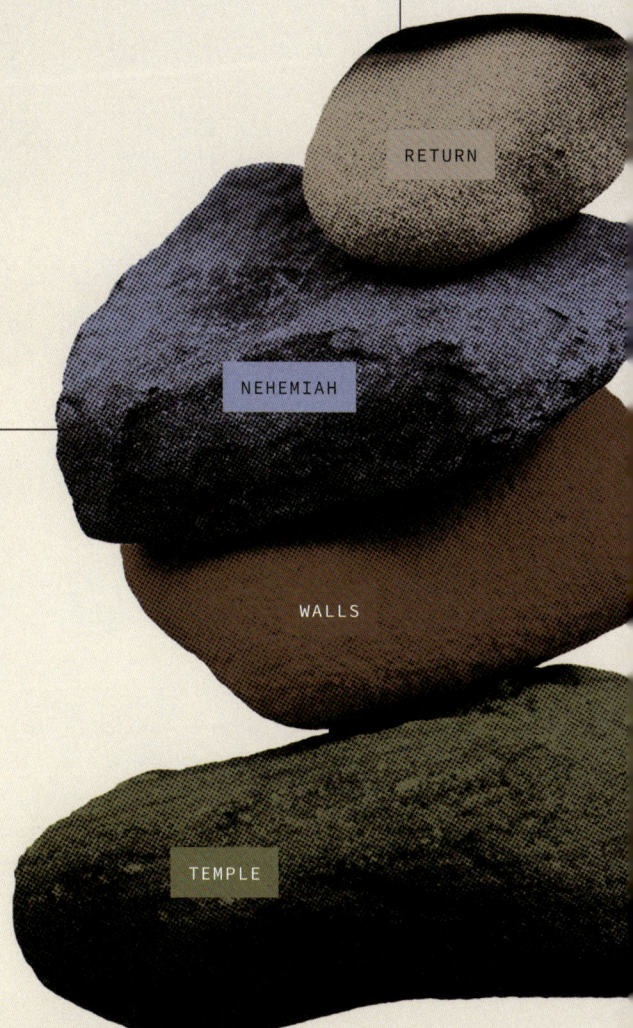

RETURN

NEHEMIAH

WALLS

458 BC

A new Persian king, Artaxerxes I, issues a decree declaring that the exiles living in Persia are free to return home.

Led by Ezra, a group of exiles return from Persia to the promised land.

Nehemiah remains in Persia, eventually becoming the royal cupbearer for King Artaxerxes.

TEMPLE

479 BC

Esther becomes queen of Persia.

© 2025 She Reads Truth. All rights reserved.

Preparing *to* Rebuild

DAY   03

Nehemiah 2:11–20

PREPARING TO REBUILD THE WALLS

[11] After I arrived in Jerusalem and had been there three days, [12] I got up at night and took a few men with me. I didn't tell anyone what my God had laid on my heart to do for Jerusalem. The only animal I took was the one I was riding. [13] I went out at night through the Valley Gate toward the Serpent's Well and the Dung Gate, and I inspected the walls of Jerusalem that had been broken down and its gates that had been destroyed by fire. [14] I went on to the Fountain Gate and the King's Pool, but farther down it became too narrow for my animal to go through. [15] So I went up at night by way of the valley and inspected the wall. Then heading back, I entered through the Valley Gate and returned. [16] The officials did not know where I had gone or what I was doing, for I had not yet told the Jews, priests, nobles, officials, or the rest of those who would be doing the work. [17] So I said to them, "You see the trouble we are in. Jerusalem lies in ruins and its gates have been burned. Come, let's rebuild Jerusalem's wall, so that we will no longer be a disgrace." [18] I told them how the gracious hand of my God had been on me, and what the king had said to me.

They said, "Let's start rebuilding," and their hands were strengthened to do this good work.

¹⁹ When Sanballat the Horonite, Tobiah the Ammonite official, and Geshem the Arab heard about this, they mocked and despised us, and said, "What is this you're doing? Are you rebelling against the king?"

²⁰ I gave them this reply, "The God of the heavens is the one who will grant us success. We, his servants, will start building, but you have no share, right, or historic claim in Jerusalem."

◆ GOING DEEPER

Isaiah 62:10–12

¹⁰ Go out, go out through the city gates;
prepare a way for the people!
Build it up, build up the highway;
clear away the stones!
Raise a banner for the peoples.
¹¹ Look, the Lord has proclaimed
to the ends of the earth,
"Say to Daughter Zion:
Look, your salvation is coming,
his wages are with him,
and his reward accompanies him."
¹² And they will be called the Holy People,
the Lord's Redeemed;
and you will be called Cared For,
A City Not Deserted.

Ephesians 2:19–22

¹⁹ So, then, you are no longer foreigners and strangers, but fellow citizens with the saints, and members of God's household, ²⁰ built on the foundation of the apostles and prophets, with Christ Jesus himself as the cornerstone. ²¹ In him the whole building, being put together, grows into a holy temple in the Lord. ²² In him you are also being built together for God's dwelling in the Spirit.

Rebuilding *the* Walls

THE HIGH PRIEST ELIASHIB AND HIS FELLOW PRIESTS BEGAN REBUILDING THE SHEEP GATE. THEY DEDICATED IT AND INSTALLED ITS DOORS. AFTER BUILDING THE WALL TO THE TOWER OF THE HUNDRED AND THE TOWER OF HANANEL, THEY DEDICATED IT.

Nehemiah 3:1

Nehemiah 3

REBUILDING THE WALLS

[1] The high priest Eliashib and his fellow priests began rebuilding the Sheep Gate. They dedicated it and installed its doors. After building the wall to the Tower of the Hundred and the Tower of Hananel, they dedicated it. [2] The men of Jericho built next to Eliashib, and next to them Zaccur son of Imri built.

FISH GATE

[3] The sons of Hassenaah built the Fish Gate. They built it with beams and installed its doors, bolts, and bars. [4] Next to them Meremoth son of Uriah, son of Hakkoz, made repairs. Beside them Meshullam son of Berechiah, son of Meshezabel, made repairs. Next to them Zadok son of Baana made repairs. [5] Beside them the Tekoites made repairs, but their nobles did not lift a finger to help their supervisors.

See "The Walls of Jerusalem in Nehemiah's Time" map on page 50 to see the locations of these gates surrounding the city.

OLD GATE, BROAD WALL, AND TOWER OF THE OVENS

[6] Joiada son of Paseah and Meshullam son of Besodeiah repaired the Old Gate. They built it with beams and installed its doors, bolts, and bars. [7] Next to them the repairs were done by Melatiah the Gibeonite, Jadon the Meronothite, and the men of Gibeon and Mizpah, who were under the authority of the governor of the region west of the Euphrates River. [8] After him Uzziel son of Harhaiah, the goldsmith, made repairs, and next to him Hananiah son of the perfumer made repairs. They restored Jerusalem as far as the Broad Wall.

[9] Next to them Rephaiah son of Hur, ruler of half the district of Jerusalem, made repairs. [10] After them Jedaiah son of Harumaph made repairs across from his house. Next to him Hattush the son of Hashabneiah made repairs. [11] Malchijah son of Harim and Hasshub son of Pahath-moab made repairs to another section, as well as to the Tower of the Ovens. [12] Beside him Shallum son of Hallohesh, ruler of half the district of Jerusalem, made repairs—he and his daughters.

VALLEY GATE, DUNG GATE, AND FOUNTAIN GATE

[13] Hanun and the inhabitants of Zanoah repaired the Valley Gate. They rebuilt it and installed its doors, bolts, and bars, and repaired five hundred yards of the wall to the Dung Gate. [14] Malchijah son of Rechab, ruler of the district of Beth-haccherem, repaired the Dung Gate. He rebuilt it and installed its doors, bolts, and bars.

[15] Shallun son of Col-hozeh, ruler of the district of Mizpah, repaired the Fountain Gate. He rebuilt it and roofed it. Then he installed its doors, bolts, and bars. He also made repairs to the wall of the Pool of Shelah near the king's garden, as far as the stairs that descend from the city of David.

[16] After him Nehemiah son of Azbuk, ruler of half the district of Beth-zur, made repairs up to a point opposite the tombs of David, as far as the artificial pool and the House of the Warriors. [17] Next to him the Levites made repairs under Rehum son of Bani. Beside him Hashabiah, ruler of half the district of Keilah, made repairs for his district. [18] After him their fellow Levites made repairs under Binnui son of Henadad, ruler of half the district of Keilah. [19] Next to him Ezer son of Jeshua, ruler of Mizpah, made repairs to another section opposite the ascent to the armory at the Angle.

THE ANGLE, WATER GATE, AND TOWER ON OPHEL

[20] After him Baruch son of Zabbai diligently repaired another section, from the Angle to the door of the house of the high priest Eliashib. [21] Beside him Meremoth son of Uriah, son of Hakkoz, made repairs to another section, from the door of Eliashib's house to the end of his house. [22] And next to him the priests from the surrounding area made repairs.

[23] After them Benjamin and Hasshub made repairs opposite their house. Beside them Azariah son of Maaseiah, son of Ananiah, made repairs beside his house. [24] After him Binnui son of Henadad made repairs to another section, from the house of Azariah to the Angle and the corner. [25] Palal son of Uzai made repairs opposite the Angle and tower that juts out from the king's upper palace, by the courtyard of the guard. Beside him Pedaiah son of Parosh [26] and the temple servants living on Ophel made repairs opposite the Water Gate toward the east and the tower that juts out. [27] Next to him the Tekoites made repairs to another section from a point opposite the great tower that juts out, as far as the wall of Ophel.

HORSE GATE, INSPECTION GATE, AND SHEEP GATE

[28] Each of the priests made repairs above the Horse Gate, each opposite his own house. [29] After them Zadok son of Immer made repairs opposite his house. And beside him Shemaiah son of Shecaniah, guard of the East Gate, made repairs. [30] Next to him Hananiah son of Shelemiah and Hanun the sixth son of Zalaph made repairs to another section.

After them Meshullam son of Berechiah made repairs opposite his room. [31] Next to him Malchijah, one of the goldsmiths, made repairs to the house of the temple servants and the merchants, opposite the Inspection Gate, and as far as the upstairs room on the corner. [32] The goldsmiths and merchants made repairs between the upstairs room on the corner and the Sheep Gate.

⬗ GOING DEEPER

Isaiah 58:11–12

[11] The Lord will always lead you,
satisfy you in a parched land,
and strengthen your bones.
You will be like a watered garden
and like a spring whose water never runs dry.
[12] Some of you will rebuild the ancient ruins;
you will restore the foundations laid long ago;
you will be called the repairer of broken walls,
the restorer of streets where people live.

Hebrews 6:7–12

[7] For the ground that drinks the rain that often falls on it and that produces vegetation useful to those for whom it is cultivated receives a blessing from God. [8] But if it produces thorns and thistles, it is worthless and about to be cursed, and at the end will be burned.

[9] Even though we are speaking this way, dearly loved friends, in your case we are confident of things that are better and that pertain to salvation. [10] For God is not unjust; he will not forget your work and the love you demonstrated for his name by serving the saints—and by continuing to serve them. [11] Now we desire each of you to demonstrate the same diligence for the full assurance of your hope until the end, [12] so that you won't become lazy but will be imitators of those who inherit the promises through faith and perseverance.

Progress *Despite Opposition*

Nehemiah 4

PROGRESS IN SPITE OF OPPOSITION

[1] When Sanballat heard that we were rebuilding the wall, he became furious. He mocked the Jews [2] before his colleagues and the powerful men of Samaria and said, "What are these pathetic Jews doing? Can they restore it by themselves? Will they offer sacrifices? Will they ever finish it? Can they bring these burnt stones back to life from the mounds of rubble?" [3] Then Tobiah the Ammonite, who was beside him, said, "Indeed, even if a fox climbed up what they are building, he would break down their stone wall!"

[4] Listen, our God, for we are despised. Make their insults return on their own heads and let them be taken as plunder to a land of captivity. [5] Do not cover their guilt or let their sin be erased from your sight, because they have angered the builders.

[6] So we rebuilt the wall until the entire wall was joined together up to half its height, for the people had the will to keep working.

[7] When Sanballat, Tobiah, and the Arabs, Ammonites, and Ashdodites heard that the repair to the walls of Jerusalem was progressing and that the gaps were being closed, they became furious. [8] They all plotted together to come and fight against Jerusalem and throw it into confusion. [9] So we prayed to our God and stationed a guard because of them day and night.

[10] In Judah, it was said:

The strength of the laborer fails,
since there is so much rubble.
We will never be able
to rebuild the wall.

[11] And our enemies said, "They won't realize it until we're among them and can kill them and stop the work." [12] When the Jews who lived nearby arrived, they said to us time and again, "Everywhere you turn, they attack us." [13] So I stationed people behind the lowest sections of the wall, at the vulnerable areas. I stationed them by families with their swords, spears, and bows. [14] After I made an inspection, I stood up and said to the nobles, the officials, and the rest of the people, "Don't be afraid of them. Remember the great and awe-inspiring Lord, and fight for your countrymen, your sons and daughters, your wives and homes."

SWORD AND TROWEL

[15] When our enemies heard that we knew their scheme and that God had frustrated it, every one of us returned to his own work on the wall. [16] From that day on, half of my men did the work while the other half held spears, shields, bows, and armor.

The officers supported all the people of Judah, [17] who were rebuilding the wall. The laborers who carried the loads worked with one hand and held a weapon with the other. [18] Each of the builders had his sword strapped around his waist while he was building, and the one who sounded the ram's horn was beside me. [19] Then I said to the nobles, the officials, and the rest of the people, "The work is enormous and spread out, and we are separated far from one another along the wall. [20] Wherever you hear the sound of the ram's horn, rally to us there. Our God will fight for us!" [21] So we continued the work, while half of the men were holding spears from daybreak until the stars came out. [22] At that time, I also said to the people, "Let everyone and his servant spend the night inside Jerusalem, so that they can stand guard by night and work by day." [23] And I, my brothers, my servants, and the men of the guard with me never took off our clothes. Each carried his weapon, even when washing.

♥ GOING DEEPER

Psalm 41:4–13

[4] I said, "LORD, be gracious to me;
heal me, for I have sinned against you."
[5] My enemies speak maliciously about me:
"When will he die and be forgotten?"
[6] When one of them comes to visit, he speaks deceitfully;
he stores up evil in his heart;
he goes out and talks.
[7] All who hate me whisper together about me;
they plan to harm me.
[8] "Something awful has overwhelmed him,
and he won't rise again from where he lies!"
[9] Even my friend in whom I trusted,
one who ate my bread,
has raised his heel against me.

[10] But you, LORD, be gracious to me and raise me up;
then I will repay them.
[11] By this I know that you delight in me:
my enemy does not shout in triumph over me.
[12] You supported me because of my integrity
and set me in your presence forever.

[13] Blessed be the LORD God of Israel,
from everlasting to everlasting.
Amen and amen.

1 Peter 5:6–11

[6] Humble yourselves, therefore, under the mighty hand of God, so that he may exalt you at the proper time, [7] casting all your cares on him, because he cares about you. [8] Be sober-minded, be alert. Your adversary the devil is prowling around like a roaring lion, looking for anyone he can devour. [9] Resist him, firm in the faith, knowing that the same kind of sufferings are being experienced by your fellow believers throughout the world.

[10] The God of all grace, who called you to his eternal glory in Christ, will himself restore, establish, strengthen, and support you after you have suffered a little while. [11] To him be dominion forever. Amen.

Day 5
Notes

Week 1
Response

Use the following questions to reflect on how the themes of
returning and rebuilding *are at work in the book of Nehemiah.*

01   Why did Nehemiah mourn the state of Jerusalem (Neh 1)?

02   How did God's people respond to Nehemiah's plan to rebuild?

03   When in your life have you felt the need to return to God, and how did you respond in that situation?

Grace Day

TAKE THIS DAY TO CATCH UP ON YOUR
READING, PRAY, AND REST IN THE
PRESENCE OF THE LORD.

And they will be
called *the* Holy People,
the LORD's Redeemed;
and you will be called
Cared For, *A* City
Not Deserted.

Isaiah 62:12

Weekly Truth

SCRIPTURE IS GOD BREATHED AND TRUE.
WHEN WE MEMORIZE IT, WE CARRY HIS
WORD WITH US WHEREVER WE GO.

THROUGHOUT THIS PLAN, WE WILL
MEMORIZE NEHEMIAH 13:22B, A REMINDER
OF GOD'S HEART TOWARD US AS WE SEEK
TO OBEY HIM. THIS WEEK, MEMORIZE THE
FIRST HALF.

SEE TIPS FOR MEMORIZING
SCRIPTURE ON PAGE 100.

*Remember me for this also,
my God,* and look on me
with compassion according
to the abundance of your
faithful love.

Nehemiah 13:22b

Social Injustice

THEN I SAID, "WHAT YOU ARE DOING ISN'T RIGHT. SHOULDN'T YOU WALK IN THE FEAR OF OUR GOD AND NOT INVITE THE REPROACH OF OUR FOREIGN ENEMIES?"

Nehemiah 5:9

Nehemiah 5

SOCIAL INJUSTICE

¹ There was a widespread outcry from the people and their wives against their Jewish countrymen. ² Some were saying, "We, our sons, and our daughters are numerous. Let us get grain so that we can eat and live." ³ Others were saying, "We are mortgaging our fields, vineyards, and homes to get grain during the famine." ⁴ Still others were saying, "We have borrowed money to pay the king's tax on our fields and vineyards. ⁵ We and our children are just like our countrymen and their children, yet we are subjecting our sons and daughters to slavery. Some of our daughters are already enslaved, but we are powerless because our fields and vineyards belong to others."

⁶ I became extremely angry when I heard their outcry and these complaints. ⁷ After seriously considering the matter, I accused the nobles and officials, saying to them, "Each of you is charging his countrymen interest." So I called a large assembly against them ⁸ and said, "We have done our best to buy back our Jewish countrymen who were sold to foreigners, but now you sell your own countrymen, and we have to buy them back." They remained silent and could not say a word. ⁹ Then I said, "What you are doing isn't right. Shouldn't you walk in the fear of our God and not invite the reproach of our foreign enemies? ¹⁰ Even I, as well as my brothers and my servants, have been lending them money and grain. Please, let's stop charging this interest. ¹¹ Return their fields, vineyards, olive groves, and houses to them immediately, along with the percentage of the money, grain, new wine, and fresh oil that you have been assessing them."

¹² They responded, "We will return these things and require nothing more from them. We will do as you say."

So I summoned the priests and made everyone take an oath to do this. ¹³ I also shook the folds of my robe and said, "May God likewise shake from his house and property everyone who doesn't keep this promise. May he be shaken out and have nothing!"

The whole assembly said, "Amen," and they praised the LORD. Then the people did as they had promised.

GOOD AND BAD GOVERNORS

¹⁴ Furthermore, from the day King Artaxerxes appointed me to be their governor in the land of Judah—from the twentieth year until his thirty-second year, twelve years—I and my associates never ate from the food allotted to the governor. ¹⁵ The governors who preceded me had heavily burdened the people, taking from them food and wine as well as a pound of silver. Their subordinates also oppressed the people, but because of the fear of God, I didn't do this. ¹⁶ Instead, I devoted myself to the construction of this wall, and all my subordinates were gathered there for the work. We didn't buy any land.

[17] There were 150 Jews and officials, as well as guests from the surrounding nations at my table. [18] Each day, one ox, six choice sheep, and some fowl were prepared for me. An abundance of all kinds of wine was provided every ten days. But I didn't demand the food allotted to the governor, because the burden on the people was so heavy.

[19] Remember me favorably, my God, for all that I have done for this people.

◗ GOING DEEPER

Deuteronomy 23:19–20

INTEREST ON LOANS

[19] Do not charge your brother interest on silver, food, or anything that can earn interest. [20] You may charge a foreigner interest, but you must not charge your brother Israelite interest, so that the LORD your God may bless you in everything you do in the land you are entering to possess.

Romans 15:1–6

PLEASING OTHERS, NOT OURSELVES

[1] Now we who are strong have an obligation to bear the weaknesses of those without strength, and not to please ourselves. [2] Each one of us is to please his neighbor for his good, to build him up. [3] For even Christ did not please himself. On the contrary, as it is written, The insults of those who insult you have fallen on me. [4] For whatever was written in the past was written for our instruction, so that we may have hope through endurance and through the encouragement from the Scriptures. [5] Now may the God who gives endurance and encouragement grant you to live in harmony with one another, according to Christ Jesus, [6] so that you may glorify the God and Father of our Lord Jesus Christ with one mind and one voice.

Day 8
Notes

THE WALL WAS COMPLETED IN FIFTY-TWO DAYS, ON THE TWENTY-FIFTH DAY OF THE MONTH ELUL. WHEN ALL OUR ENEMIES HEARD THIS, ALL THE SURROUNDING NATIONS WERE INTIMIDATED AND LOST THEIR CONFIDENCE, FOR THEY REALIZED THAT THIS TASK HAD BEEN ACCOMPLISHED BY OUR GOD.

Nehemiah 6:15–16

The Wall Completed

Nehemiah 6

ATTEMPTS TO DISCOURAGE THE BUILDERS

¹ When Sanballat, Tobiah, Geshem the Arab, and the rest of our enemies heard that I had rebuilt the wall and that no gap was left in it—though at that time I had not installed the doors in the city gates— ² Sanballat and Geshem sent me a message: "Come, let's meet together in the villages of the Ono Valley." They were planning to harm me.

³ So I sent messengers to them, saying, "I am doing important work and cannot come down. Why should the work cease while I leave it and go down to you?" ⁴ Four times they sent me the same proposal, and I gave them the same reply.

⁵ Sanballat sent me this same message a fifth time by his aide, who had an open letter in his hand. ⁶ In it was written:

It is reported among the nations—and Geshem agrees—that you and the Jews plan to rebel. This is the reason you are building the wall. According to these reports, you are to become their king ⁷ and have even set up the prophets in Jerusalem to proclaim on your behalf, "There is a king in Judah." These rumors will be heard by the king. So come, let's confer together.

⁸ Then I replied to him, "There is nothing to these rumors you are spreading; you are inventing them in your own mind." ⁹ For they were all trying to intimidate us, saying, "They will drop their hands from the work, and it will never be finished."

But now, my God, strengthen my hands.

ATTEMPTS TO INTIMIDATE NEHEMIAH

¹⁰ I went to the house of Shemaiah son of Delaiah, son of Mehetabel, who was restricted to his house. He said:

In the book of Nehemiah, God's people are referenced as both *Israelites* and *Jews*.

After some of the exiles began returning from Babylon to the land that was previously known as the southern kingdom of Judah, they were collectively known as *Judahites*.

The religion practiced by those who returned from exile became known as *Judaism*.

The Greek name for the region of Judah was *Judea* (Mt 2:1), and the land itself and the people living there were described as "Judean" (Mk 1:5). *Judean* eventually became shortened to the first syllable, "Jew."

Let's meet at the house of God,
inside the temple.
Let's shut the temple doors
because they're coming to kill you.
They're coming to kill you tonight!

[11] But I said, "Should a man like me run away? How can someone like me enter the temple and live? I will not go." [12] I realized that God had not sent him, because of the prophecy he spoke against me. Tobiah and Sanballat had hired him. [13] He was hired, so that I would be intimidated, do as he suggested, sin, and get a bad reputation, in order that they could discredit me.

[14] My God, remember Tobiah and Sanballat for what they have done, and also the prophetess Noadiah and the other prophets who wanted to intimidate me.

THE WALL COMPLETED

[15] The wall was completed in fifty-two days, on the twenty-fifth day of the month Elul. [16] When all our enemies heard this, all the surrounding nations were intimidated and lost their confidence, for they realized that this task had been accomplished by our God.

[17] During those days, the nobles of Judah sent many letters to Tobiah, and Tobiah's letters came to them. [18] For many in Judah were bound by oath to him, since he was a son-in-law of Shecaniah son of Arah, and his son Jehohanan had married the daughter of Meshullam son of Berechiah. [19] These nobles kept mentioning Tobiah's good deeds to me, and they reported my words to him. And Tobiah sent letters to intimidate me.

♥ GOING DEEPER

Isaiah 40:9–11, 28–31

[9] Zion, herald of good news,
go up on a high mountain.
Jerusalem, herald of good news,
raise your voice loudly.
Raise it, do not be afraid!
Say to the cities of Judah,
"Here is your God!"
[10] See, the Lord GOD comes with strength,
and his power establishes his rule.
His wages are with him,
and his reward accompanies him.

[11] He protects his flock like a shepherd;
he gathers the lambs in his arms
and carries them in the fold of his garment.
He gently leads those that are nursing.

…

[28] Do you not know?
Have you not heard?
The LORD is the everlasting God,
the Creator of the whole earth.
He never becomes faint or weary;
there is no limit to his understanding.
[29] He gives strength to the faint
and strengthens the powerless.
[30] Youths may become faint and weary,
and young men stumble and fall,
[31] but those who trust in the LORD
will renew their strength;
they will soar on wings like eagles;
they will run and not become weary,
they will walk and not faint.

2 Timothy 4:17–18

[17] But the Lord stood with me and strengthened me, so that I might fully preach the word and all the Gentiles might hear it. So I was rescued from the lion's mouth. [18] The Lord will rescue me from every evil work and will bring me safely into his heavenly kingdom. To him be the glory forever and ever! Amen.

The Walls

of

Jerusalem

in Nehemiah's Time

The following map displays the rebuilt walls of Jerusalem, along with the key gates and features detailed in the book of Nehemiah. Use this map as a visual aid to supplement your reading of the detailed building project.

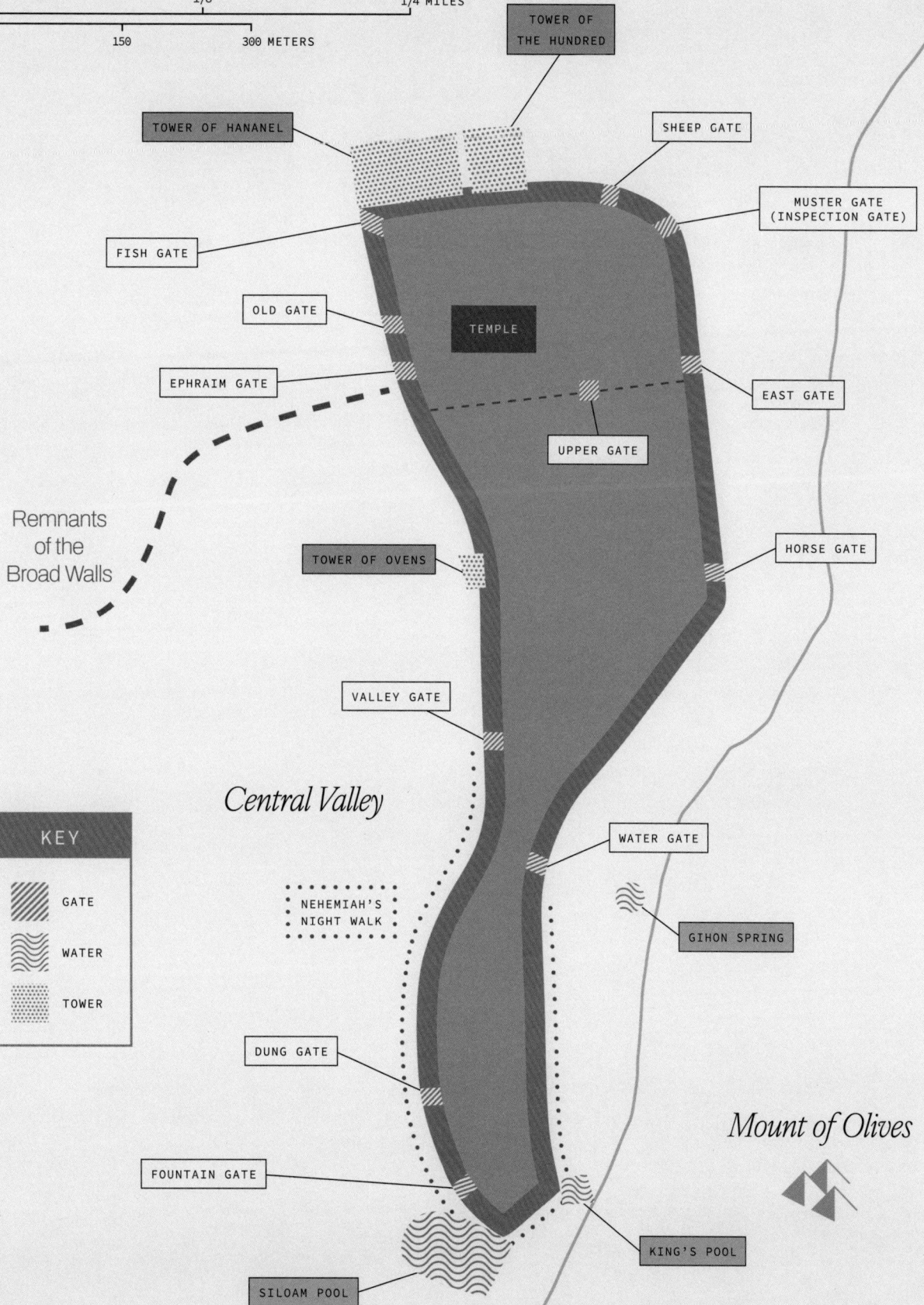

© 2018, 2025 She Reads Truth. All rights reserved.

0   1/8   1/4 MILES

0   150   300 METERS

TOWER OF
THE HUNDRED

TOWER OF HANANEL

SHEEP GATE

MUSTER GATE
(INSPECTION GATE)

FISH GATE

OLD GATE

TEMPLE

EPHRAIM GATE

EAST GATE

UPPER GATE

Remnants
of the
Broad Walls

HORSE GATE

TOWER OF OVENS

VALLEY GATE

Central Valley

WATER GATE

KEY

GATE

WATER

TOWER

NEHEMIAH'S
NIGHT WALK

GIHON SPRING

DUNG GATE

Mount of Olives

FOUNTAIN GATE

KING'S POOL

SILOAM POOL

The Exiles Returned

THE PRIESTS, LEVITES, GATEKEEPERS, TEMPLE
SINGERS, SOME OF THE PEOPLE, TEMPLE SERVANTS,
AND ALL ISRAEL SETTLED IN THEIR TOWNS.

Nehemiah 7:73

Nehemiah 7:1–73a

THE EXILES RETURN

¹ When the wall had been rebuilt and I had the doors installed, the gatekeepers, singers, and Levites were appointed. ² Then I put my brother Hanani in charge of Jerusalem, along with Hananiah, commander of the fortress, because he was a faithful man who feared God more than most. ³ I said to them, "Do not open the gates of Jerusalem until the sun is hot, and let the doors be shut and securely fastened while the guards are on duty. Station the citizens of Jerusalem as guards, some at their posts and some at their homes."

⁴ The city was large and spacious, but there were few people in it, and no houses had been built yet. ⁵ Then my God put it into my mind to assemble the nobles, the officials, and the people to be registered by genealogy. I found the genealogical record of those who came back first, and I found the following written in it:

⁶ These are the people of the province who went up among the captive exiles deported by King Nebuchadnezzar of Babylon. Each of them returned to Jerusalem and Judah, to his own town. ⁷ They came with Zerubbabel, Jeshua, Nehemiah, Azariah, Raamiah, Nahamani, Mordecai, Bilshan, Mispereth, Bigvai, Nehum, and Baanah.

This list of returnees almost exactly matches the list recorded in Ezra 2, which would likely have been the earliest group of exiles King Cyrus released in 538 BC. As Nehemiah and other leadership worked to reorient the nation to the truth of God's law, Nehemiah likely referenced the earlier census to recall familial lineage since it was necessary to legitimize the Levites' calling and priestly responsibility for this new generation of God's people.

The number of the Israelite men included

[8] Parosh's descendants	2,172
[9] Shephatiah's descendants	372
[10] Arah's descendants	652
[11] Pahath-moab's descendants:	
Jeshua's and Joab's descendants	2,818
[12] Elam's descendants	1,254
[13] Zattu's descendants	845
[14] Zaccai's descendants	760
[15] Binnui's descendants	648
[16] Bebai's descendants	628
[17] Azgad's descendants	2,322
[18] Adonikam's descendants	667
[19] Bigvai's descendants	2,067
[20] Adin's descendants	655
[21] Ater's descendants: of Hezekiah	98
[22] Hashum's descendants	328
[23] Bezai's descendants	324
[24] Hariph's descendants	112
[25] Gibeon's descendants	95
[26] Bethlehem's and Netophah's men	188
[27] Anathoth's men	128
[28] Beth-azmaveth's men	42
[29] Kiriath-jearim's, Chephirah's, and Beeroth's men	743
[30] Ramah's and Geba's men	621
[31] Michmas's men	122
[32] Bethel's and Ai's men	123
[33] the other Nebo's men	52
[34] the other Elam's people	1,254
[35] Harim's people	320
[36] Jericho's people	345
[37] Lod's, Hadid's, and Ono's people	721
[38] Senaah's people	3,930.

[39] The priests included

Jedaiah's descendants of the house of Jeshua	973
[40] Immer's descendants	1,052
[41] Pashhur's descendants	1,247
[42] Harim's descendants	1,017.

[43] The Levites included

Jeshua's descendants: of Kadmiel	
Hodevah's descendants	74.

[44] The singers included

Asaph's descendants	148.

[45] The gatekeepers included

Shallum's descendants, Ater's descendants, Talmon's descendants, Akkub's descendants, Hatita's descendants, Shobai's descendants	138.

[46] The temple servants included

Ziha's descendants, Hasupha's descendants, Tabbaoth's descendants, [47] Keros's descendants, Sia's descendants, Padon's descendants, [48] Lebanah's descendants, Hagabah's descendants, Shalmai's descendants, [49] Hanan's descendants, Giddel's descendants, Gahar's descendants, [50] Reaiah's descendants, Rezin's descendants, Nekoda's descendants, [51] Gazzam's descendants, Uzza's descendants, Paseah's descendants, [52] Besai's descendants, Meunim's descendants, Nephishesim's descendants, [53] Bakbuk's descendants, Hakupha's descendants, Harhur's descendants, [54] Bazlith's descendants, Mehida's descendants, Harsha's descendants, [55] Barkos's descendants, Sisera's descendants, Temah's descendants, [56] Neziah's descendants, Hatipha's descendants.

[57] The descendants of Solomon's servants included

Sotai's descendants, Sophereth's descendants, Perida's descendants, [58] Jaala's descendants, Darkon's descendants, Giddel's descendants, [59] Shephatiah's descendants, Hattil's descendants, Pochereth-hazzebaim's descendants, Amon's descendants.

60 All the temple servants
and the descendants of Solomon's servants   392.

61 The following are those who came from Tel-melah, Tel-harsha, Cherub, Addon, and Immer, but were unable to prove that their ancestral families and their lineage were Israelite:

62 Delaiah's descendants,
Tobiah's descendants,
and Nekoda's descendants   642

63 and from the priests: the descendants of Hobaiah, the descendants of Hakkoz, and the descendants of Barzillai—who had taken a wife from the daughters of Barzillai the Gileadite and who bore their name. 64 These searched for their entries in the genealogical records, but they could not be found, so they were disqualified from the priesthood. 65 The governor ordered them not to eat the most holy things until there was a priest who could consult the Urim and Thummim.

66 The whole combined assembly numbered   42,360
67 not including their 7,337 male and female servants,
as well as their 245 male and female singers.
68 They had 736 horses, 245 mules,
69 435 camels, and 6,720 donkeys.

70 Some of the family heads contributed to the project. The governor gave 1,000 gold coins, 50 bowls, and 530 priestly garments to the treasury. 71 Some of the family heads gave 20,000 gold coins and 2,200 silver minas to the treasury for the project. 72 The rest of the people gave 20,000 gold coins, 2,000 silver minas, and 67 priestly garments. 73 The priests, Levites, gatekeepers, temple singers, some of the people, temple servants, and all Israel settled in their towns.

◆ GOING DEEPER

Psalm 122

A PRAYER FOR JERUSALEM

A song of ascents. Of David.

1 I rejoiced with those who said to me,
"Let's go to the house of the LORD."
2 Our feet were standing
within your gates, Jerusalem—

3 Jerusalem, built as a city should be,
solidly united,
4 where the tribes, the LORD's tribes, go up
to give thanks to the name of the LORD.
(This is an ordinance for Israel.)
5 There, thrones for judgment are placed,
thrones of the house of David.

6 Pray for the well-being of Jerusalem:
"May those who love you be secure;
7 may there be peace within your walls,
security within your fortresses."
8 Because of my brothers and friends,
I will say, "May peace be in you."
9 Because of the house of the LORD our God,
I will pursue your prosperity.

Public Reading
of the Law

Nehemiah 7:73b

PUBLIC READING OF THE LAW

When the seventh month came and the Israelites had settled in their towns,

Nehemiah 8

¹ all the people gathered together at the square in front of the Water Gate. They asked the scribe Ezra to bring the book of the law of Moses that the LORD had given Israel. ² On the first day of the seventh month, the priest Ezra brought the law before the assembly of men, women, and all who could listen with understanding. ³ While he was facing the square in front of the Water Gate, he read out of it from daybreak until noon before the men, the women, and those who could understand. All the people listened attentively to the book of the law. ⁴ The scribe Ezra stood on a high wooden platform made for this purpose. Mattithiah, Shema, Anaiah, Uriah, Hilkiah, and Maaseiah stood beside him on his right; to his left were Pedaiah, Mishael, Malchijah, Hashum, Hash-baddanah, Zechariah, and Meshullam. ⁵ Ezra opened the book in full view of all the people, since he was elevated above everyone. As he opened it, all the people stood up. ⁶ Ezra blessed the LORD, the great God, and with their hands uplifted all the people said, "Amen, Amen!" Then they knelt low and worshiped the LORD with their faces to the ground.

⁷ Jeshua, Bani, Sherebiah, Jamin, Akkub, Shabbethai, Hodiah, Maaseiah, Kelita, Azariah, Jozabad, Hanan, and Pelaiah, who were Levites, explained the law to the people as they stood in their places. ⁸ They read out of the book of the law of God, translating and giving the meaning so that the people could understand what was read. ⁹ Nehemiah the governor, Ezra the priest and scribe, and the Levites who were instructing the people said to all of them, "This day is holy to the LORD your God. Do not mourn or weep." For all the people were weeping as they heard the words of the law. ¹⁰ Then he said to them, "Go and eat what is rich, drink what is sweet, and send portions to those who have nothing prepared, since today is holy to our Lord. Do not grieve, because the joy of the LORD is your strength." ¹¹ And the Levites quieted all the people, saying, "Be still, since today is holy. Don't grieve." ¹² Then all the people began to eat and drink, send portions, and have a great celebration, because they had understood the words that were explained to them.

FESTIVAL OF SHELTERS OBSERVED

¹³ On the second day, the family heads of all the people, along with the priests and Levites, assembled before the scribe Ezra to study the words of the law. ¹⁴ They found written in the law how the LORD had commanded through Moses that the Israelites should dwell in shelters during the festival of the seventh month. ¹⁵ So they proclaimed and spread this news throughout their towns and in Jerusalem, saying, "Go out to the hill country and bring back branches of olive, wild olive, myrtle, palm, and other leafy trees to make shelters, just as it is written." ¹⁶ The

> Though we don't know how much of the law was read, the text highlights the goal of helping the people hear, understand, and reorder their lives around the law (Neh 8:1-2, 7-8). The helpers and Levites named were there to aid Ezra in possibly translating and/or explaining the law of Moses as it was read.

people went out, brought back branches, and made shelters for themselves on each of their rooftops and courtyards, the court of the house of God, the square by the Water Gate, and the square by the Ephraim Gate. ¹⁷ The whole community that had returned from exile made shelters and lived in them. The Israelites had not celebrated like this from the days of Joshua son of Nun until that day. And there was tremendous joy. ¹⁸ Ezra read out of the book of the law of God every day, from the first day to the last. The Israelites celebrated the festival for seven days, and on the eighth day there was a solemn assembly, according to the ordinance.

◆ GOING DEEPER

Deuteronomy 10:12–22
WHAT GOD REQUIRES

¹² And now, Israel, what does the LORD your God ask of you except to fear the LORD your God by walking in all his ways, to love him, and to worship the LORD your God with all your heart and all your soul? ¹³ Keep the LORD's commands and statutes I am giving you today, for your own good. ¹⁴ The heavens, indeed the highest heavens, belong to the LORD your God, as does the earth and everything in it. ¹⁵ Yet the LORD had his heart set on your ancestors and loved them. He chose their descendants after them—he chose you out of all the peoples, as it is today. ¹⁶ Therefore, circumcise your hearts and don't be stiff-necked any longer. ¹⁷ For the LORD your God is the God of gods and Lord of lords, the great, mighty, and awe-inspiring God, showing no partiality and taking no bribe. ¹⁸ He executes justice for the fatherless and the widow, and loves the resident alien, giving him food and clothing. ¹⁹ You are also to love the resident alien, since you were resident aliens in the land of Egypt. ²⁰ You are to fear the LORD your God and worship him. Remain faithful to him and take oaths in his name. ²¹ He is your praise and he is your God, who has done for you these great and awe-inspiring works your eyes have seen. ²² Your ancestors went down to Egypt, seventy people in all, and now the LORD your God has made you numerous, like the stars of the sky.

1 John 2:3–6
GOD'S COMMANDS

³ This is how we know that we know him: if we keep his commands. ⁴ The one who says, "I have come to know him," and yet doesn't keep his commands, is a liar, and the truth is not in him. ⁵ But whoever keeps his word, truly in him the love of God is made complete. This is how we know we are in him: ⁶ The one who says he remains in him should walk just as he walked.

Day 11
Notes

Nehemiah 9:1–37

NATIONAL CONFESSION OF SIN

¹ On the twenty-fourth day of this month the Israelites assembled; they were fasting, wearing sackcloth, and had put dust on their heads. ² Those of Israelite descent separated themselves from all foreigners, and they stood and confessed their sins and the iniquities of their ancestors. ³ While thewy stood in their places, they read from the book of the law of the LORD their God for a fourth of the day and spent another fourth of the day in confession and worship of the LORD their God. ⁴ Jeshua, Bani, Kadmiel, Shebaniah, Bunni, Sherebiah, Bani, and Chenani stood on the raised platform built for the Levites and cried out loudly to the LORD their God. ⁵ Then the Levites—Jeshua, Kadmiel, Bani, Hashabneiah, Sherebiah, Hodiah, Shebaniah, and Pethahiah—said, "Stand up. Blessed be the LORD your God from everlasting to everlasting."

Blessed be your glorious name,
and may it be exalted above all blessing and praise.
⁶ You, LORD, are the only God.
You created the heavens,
the highest heavens with all their stars,
the earth and all that is on it,
the seas and all that is in them.
You give life to all of them,
and all the stars of heaven worship you.
⁷ You, the LORD,
are the God who chose Abram
and brought him out of Ur of the Chaldeans,
and changed his name to Abraham.
⁸ You found his heart faithful in your sight,
and made a covenant with him
to give the land of the Canaanites,
Hethites, Amorites, Perizzites,
Jebusites, and Girgashites—
to give it to his descendants.
You have fulfilled your promise,
for you are righteous.

⁹ You saw the oppression of our ancestors in Egypt
and heard their cry at the Red Sea.
¹⁰ You performed signs and wonders against Pharaoh,
all his officials, and all the people of his land,
for you knew how arrogantly they treated our ancestors.
You made a name for yourself
that endures to this day.

[11] You divided the sea before them,
and they crossed through it on dry ground.
You hurled their pursuers into the depths
like a stone into raging water.
[12] You led them with a pillar of cloud by day,
and with a pillar of fire by night,
to illuminate the way they should go.
[13] You came down on Mount Sinai,
and spoke to them from heaven.
You gave them impartial ordinances, reliable instructions,
and good statutes and commands.
[14] You revealed your holy Sabbath to them,
and gave them commands, statutes, and instruction
through your servant Moses.
[15] You provided bread from heaven for their hunger;
you brought them water from the rock for their thirst.
You told them to go in and possess the land
you had sworn to give them.

[16] But our ancestors acted arrogantly;
they became stiff-necked and did not listen to your commands.
[17] They refused to listen
and did not remember your wonders
you performed among them.
They became stiff-necked and appointed a leader
to return to their slavery in Egypt.
But you are a forgiving God,
gracious and compassionate,
slow to anger and abounding in faithful love,
and you did not abandon them.
[18] Even after they had cast an image of a calf
for themselves and said,
"This is your god who brought you out of Egypt,"
and they had committed terrible blasphemies,
[19] you did not abandon them in the wilderness
because of your great compassion.
During the day the pillar of cloud
never turned away from them,
guiding them on their journey.
And during the night the pillar of fire
illuminated the way they should go.
[20] You sent your good Spirit to instruct them.
You did not withhold your manna from their mouths,
and you gave them water for their thirst.

²¹ You provided for them in the wilderness forty years,
and they lacked nothing.
Their clothes did not wear out,
and their feet did not swell.

²² You gave them kingdoms and peoples
and established boundaries for them.
They took possession
of the land of King Sihon of Heshbon
and of the land of King Og of Bashan.
²³ You multiplied their descendants
like the stars of the sky
and brought them to the land
you told their ancestors to go in and possess.
²⁴ So their descendants went in and possessed the land:
You subdued the Canaanites who inhabited the land
    before them
and handed their kings and the surrounding peoples
    over to them,
to do as they pleased with them.
²⁵ They captured fortified cities and fertile land
and took possession of well-supplied houses,
cisterns cut out of rock, vineyards,
olive groves, and fruit trees in abundance.
They ate, were filled,
became prosperous, and delighted in your great goodness.

²⁶ But they were disobedient and rebelled against you.
They flung your law behind their backs
and killed your prophets
who warned them
in order to turn them back to you.
They committed terrible blasphemies.
²⁷ So you handed them over to their enemies,
who oppressed them.
In their time of distress, they cried out to you,
and you heard from heaven.
In your abundant compassion
you gave them deliverers, who rescued them
from the power of their enemies.
²⁸ But as soon as they had relief,
they again did what was evil in your sight.
So you abandoned them to the power of their enemies,
who dominated them.

When they cried out to you again,
you heard from heaven and rescued them
many times in your compassion.
²⁹ You warned them to turn back to your law,
but they acted arrogantly
and would not obey your commands.
They sinned against your ordinances,
which a person will live by if he does them.
They stubbornly resisted,
stiffened their necks, and would not obey.
³⁰ You were patient with them for many years,
and your Spirit warned them through your prophets,
but they would not listen.
Therefore, you handed them over to the
    surrounding peoples.
³¹ However, in your abundant compassion,
you did not destroy them or abandon them,
for you are a gracious and compassionate God.

³² So now, our God—the great, mighty,
and awe-inspiring God who keeps his
    gracious covenant—
do not view lightly all the hardships that have afflicted us,
our kings and leaders,
our priests and prophets,
our ancestors and all your people,
from the days of the Assyrian kings until today.
³³ You are righteous concerning all that has happened
    to us,
because you have acted faithfully,
while we have acted wickedly.
³⁴ Our kings, leaders, priests, and ancestors
did not obey your law
or listen to your commands
and warnings you gave them.
³⁵ When they were in their kingdom,
with your abundant goodness that you gave them,
and in the spacious and fertile land you set before them,
they would not serve you or turn from their wicked ways.

³⁶ Here we are today,
slaves in the land you gave our ancestors
so that they could enjoy its fruit and its goodness.
Here we are—slaves in it!

37 Its abundant harvest goes to the kings
you have set over us,
because of our sins.
They rule over our bodies
and our livestock as they please.
We are in great distress.

♥ GOING DEEPER

Hebrews 13:15

Therefore, through him let us continually offer up to God a sacrifice of praise,
that is, the fruit of lips that confess his name.

Week 2
Response

Use the following questions to reflect on how the theme of
endurance through opposition *is at work in the book of Nehemiah.*

01   What kinds of challenges and obstacles did God's people experience as they rebuilt and resettled Jerusalem?

02   How did Nehemiah and the nation of Israel respond to the internal and external opposition and threats?

03   How does their response encourage or challenge you as you navigate opposition in your own life?

Grace Day

TAKE THIS DAY TO CATCH UP ON YOUR
READING, PRAY, AND REST IN THE
PRESENCE OF THE LORD.

Yet *the* Lord had his heart set on your ancestors *and* loved them. He chose their descendants after them—he chose you out of all *the* peoples, as it is today.

Deuteronomy 10:15

Weekly Truth

SCRIPTURE IS GOD BREATHED AND TRUE.
WHEN WE MEMORIZE IT, WE CARRY HIS
WORD WITH US WHEREVER WE GO.

THROUGHOUT THIS PLAN, WE ARE
MEMORIZING NEHEMIAH 13:22B, A
REMINDER OF GOD'S HEART TOWARD US
AS WE SEEK TO OBEY HIM. THIS WEEK,
MEMORIZE THE SECOND HALF.

SEE TIPS FOR MEMORIZING
SCRIPTURE ON PAGE 100.

Remember me for this also, my God, *and look on me with compassion according to the abundance of your faithful love.*

Nehemiah 13:22b

Israel's Vow

DAY   15

Nehemiah 9:38

ISRAEL'S VOW OF FAITHFULNESS

In view of all this, we are making a binding agreement in writing on a sealed document containing the names of our leaders, Levites, and priests.

Nehemiah 10

[1] Those whose seals were on the document were

the governor Nehemiah son of Hacaliah, and Zedekiah,
[2] Seraiah, Azariah, Jeremiah,
[3] Pashhur, Amariah, Malchijah,
[4] Hattush, Shebaniah, Malluch,
[5] Harim, Meremoth, Obadiah,
[6] Daniel, Ginnethon, Baruch,
[7] Meshullam, Abijah, Mijamin,
[8] Maaziah, Bilgai, and Shemaiah.
These were the priests.
[9] The Levites were
Jeshua son of Azaniah,
Binnui of the sons of Henadad, Kadmiel,
[10] and their brothers
Shebaniah, Hodiah, Kelita, Pelaiah, Hanan,
[11] Mica, Rehob, Hashabiah,
[12] Zaccur, Sherebiah, Shebaniah,

¹³ Hodiah, Bani, and Beninu.

¹⁴ The heads of the people were
Parosh, Pahath-moab, Elam, Zattu, Bani,

¹⁵ Bunni, Azgad, Bebai,

¹⁶ Adonijah, Bigvai, Adin,

¹⁷ Ater, Hezekiah, Azzur,

¹⁸ Hodiah, Hashum, Bezai,

¹⁹ Hariph, Anathoth, Nebai,

²⁰ Magpiash, Meshullam, Hezir,

²¹ Meshezabel, Zadok, Jaddua,

²² Pelatiah, Hanan, Anaiah,

²³ Hoshea, Hananiah, Hasshub,

²⁴ Hallohesh, Pilha, Shobek,

²⁵ Rehum, Hashabnah, Maaseiah,

²⁶ Ahijah, Hanan, Anan,

²⁷ Malluch, Harim, Baanah.

²⁸ The rest of the people—the priests, Levites, gatekeepers, singers, and temple servants, along with their wives, sons, and daughters, everyone who is able to understand and who has separated themselves from the surrounding peoples to obey the law of God— ²⁹ join with their noble brothers and commit themselves with a sworn oath to follow the law of God given through God's servant Moses and to obey carefully all the commands, ordinances, and statutes of the LORD our Lord.

DETAILS OF THE VOW

³⁰ We will not give our daughters in marriage to the surrounding peoples and will not take their daughters as wives for our sons.

³¹ When the surrounding peoples bring merchandise or any kind of grain to sell on the Sabbath day, we will not buy from them on the Sabbath or a holy day. We will also leave the land uncultivated in the seventh year and will cancel every debt.

³² We will impose the following commands on ourselves:

To give an eighth of an ounce of silver yearly for the service of the house of our God: ³³ the bread displayed before the LORD, the daily grain offering, the regular burnt offering, the Sabbath and New Moon offerings, the appointed festivals, the holy things, the sin offerings to atone for Israel, and for all the work of the house of our God.

³⁴ We have cast lots among the priests, Levites, and people for the donation of wood by our ancestral families at the appointed times each year. They are to bring the wood to our God's house to burn on the altar of the LORD our God, as it is written in the law.

³⁵ We will bring the firstfruits of our land and of every fruit tree to the Lᴏʀᴅ's house year by year. ³⁶ We will also bring the firstborn of our sons and our livestock, as prescribed by the law, and will bring the firstborn of our herds and flocks to the house of our God, to the priests who serve in our God's house. ³⁷ We will bring a loaf from our first batch of dough to the priests at the storerooms of the house of our God. We will also bring the firstfruits of our grain offerings, of every fruit tree, and of the new wine and fresh oil. A tenth of our land's produce belongs to the Levites, for the Levites are to collect the one-tenth offering in all our agricultural towns. ³⁸ A priest from Aaron's descendants is to accompany the Levites when they collect the tenth, and the Levites are to take a tenth of this offering to the storerooms of the treasury in the house of our God. ³⁹ For the Israelites and the Levites are to bring the contributions of grain, new wine, and fresh oil to the storerooms where the articles of the sanctuary are kept and where the priests who minister are, along with the gatekeepers and singers. We will not neglect the house of our God.

◆ GOING DEEPER

Zechariah 10:6–12

⁶ I will strengthen the house of Judah
and deliver the house of Joseph.
I will restore them
because I have compassion on them,
and they will be
as though I had never rejected them.
For I am the Lᴏʀᴅ their God,
and I will answer them.
⁷ Ephraim will be like a warrior,
and their hearts will be glad as if with wine.
Their children will see it and be glad;
their hearts will rejoice in the Lᴏʀᴅ.

⁸ I will whistle and gather them
because I have redeemed them;
they will be as numerous as they once were.
⁹ Though I sow them among the nations,
they will remember me in the distant lands;
they and their children will live and return.
¹⁰ I will bring them back from the land of Egypt
and gather them from Assyria.
I will bring them to the land of Gilead
and to Lebanon,
but it will not be enough for them.
¹¹ The Lᴏʀᴅ will pass through the sea of distress
and strike the waves of the sea;
all the depths of the Nile will dry up.
The pride of Assyria will be brought down,
and the scepter of Egypt will come to an end.
¹² I will strengthen them in the Lᴏʀᴅ,
and they will march in his name—

this is the Lᴏʀᴅ's declaration.

Romans 6:16–19

¹⁶ Don't you know that if you offer yourselves to someone as obedient slaves, you are slaves of that one you obey—either of sin leading to death or of obedience leading to righteousness? ¹⁷ But thank God that, although you used to be slaves of sin, you obeyed from the heart that pattern of teaching to which you were handed over, ¹⁸ and having been set free from sin, you became enslaved to righteousness. ¹⁹ I am using a human analogy because of the weakness of your flesh. For just as you offered the parts of yourselves as slaves to impurity, and to greater and greater lawlessness, so now offer them as slaves to righteousness, which results in sanctification.

Day 15
Notes

Resettling Jerusalem

THE PEOPLE BLESSED ALL THE MEN WHO VOLUNTEERED TO LIVE IN JERUSALEM.

Nehemiah 11:2

Nehemiah 11:1–21

RESETTLING JERUSALEM

[1] Now the leaders of the people stayed in Jerusalem, and the rest of the people cast lots for one out of ten to come and live in Jerusalem, the holy city, while the other nine-tenths remained in their towns. [2] The people blessed all the men who volunteered to live in Jerusalem.

[3] These are the heads of the province who stayed in Jerusalem (but in the villages of Judah each lived on his own property in their towns—the Israelites, priests, Levites, temple servants, and descendants of Solomon's servants— [4] while some of the descendants of Judah and Benjamin settled in Jerusalem):

Judah's descendants:

Athaiah son of Uzziah, son of Zechariah, son of Amariah, son of Shephatiah, son of Mahalalel, of Perez's descendants; [5] and Maaseiah son of Baruch, son of Col-hozeh, son of Hazaiah, son of Adaiah, son of Joiarib, son of Zechariah, a descendant of the Shilonite. [6] The total number of Perez's descendants, who settled in Jerusalem, was 468 capable men.

[7] These were Benjamin's descendants:

Sallu son of Meshullam, son of Joed, son of Pedaiah, son of Kolaiah, son of Maaseiah, son of Ithiel, son of Jeshaiah, [8] and after him Gabbai and Sallai: 928. [9] Joel son of Zichri was the officer over them, and Judah son of Hassenuah was second in command over the city.

[10] The priests:

Jedaiah son of Joiarib, Jachin, and [11] Seraiah son of Hilkiah, son of Meshullam, son of Zadok, son of Meraioth, son of Ahitub, the chief official of God's temple, [12] and their relatives who did the work at the temple: 822. Adaiah son of Jeroham, son of Pelaliah, son of Amzi, son of Zechariah, son of Pashhur, son of Malchijah [13] and his relatives, the heads of families: 242. Amashsai son of Azarel, son of Ahzai, son of Meshillemoth, son of Immer, [14] and their relatives, capable men: 128. Zabdiel son of Haggedolim, was their chief.

[15] The Levites:

Shemaiah son of Hasshub, son of Azrikam, son of Hashabiah, son of Bunni; [16] and Shabbethai and Jozabad, from the heads of the Levites, who supervised the work outside the house of God; [17] Mattaniah son of Mica, son of Zabdi, son of Asaph, the one who began the thanksgiving in prayer; Bakbukiah, second among his relatives; and Abda son of Shammua, son of Galal, son of Jeduthun. [18] All the Levites in the holy city: 284.

¹⁹ The gatekeepers:

Akkub, Talmon, and their relatives, who guarded the city gates: 172.

²⁰ The rest of Israel, the priests, and the Levites were in all the villages of Judah, each on his own inherited property. ²¹ The temple servants lived on Ophel; Ziha and Gishpa supervised the temple servants.

◆ GOING DEEPER

Psalm 87

ZION, THE CITY OF GOD

A psalm of the sons of Korah. A song.

¹ The city he founded is on the holy mountains.
² The Lord loves Zion's city gates
more than all the dwellings of Jacob.
³ Glorious things are said about you,
city of God.   *Selah*

⁴ "I will make a record of those who know me:
Rahab, Babylon, Philistia, Tyre, and Cush—
each one was born there."
⁵ And it will be said of Zion,
"This one and that one were born in her."
The Most High himself will establish her.
⁶ When he registers the peoples,
the Lord will record,
"This one was born there."   *Selah*
⁷ Singers and dancers alike will say,
"My whole source of joy is in you."

Zephaniah 3:14–20

¹⁴ Sing for joy, Daughter Zion;
shout loudly, Israel!
Be glad and celebrate with all your heart,
Daughter Jerusalem!
¹⁵ The Lord has removed your punishment;
he has turned back your enemy.
The King of Israel, the Lord, is among you;
you need no longer fear harm.
¹⁶ On that day it will be said to Jerusalem:
"Do not fear;
Zion, do not let your hands grow weak.
¹⁷ The Lord your God is among you,
a warrior who saves.
He will rejoice over you with gladness.
He will be quiet in his love.
He will delight in you with singing."

¹⁸ I will gather those who have been driven
from the appointed festivals;
they will be a tribute from you
and a reproach on her.
¹⁹ Yes, at that time
I will deal with all who oppress you.
I will save the lame and gather the outcasts;
I will make those who were disgraced
throughout the earth
receive praise and fame.
²⁰ At that time I will bring you back,
yes, at the time I will gather you.
I will give you fame and praise
among all the peoples of the earth,
when I restore your fortunes before your eyes.
The Lord has spoken.

Day 16
Notes

Ezra *and* Nehemiah

Until about the third century AD, the books of Ezra and Nehemiah were considered a single text. Together, they record the Jewish people's return to Jerusalem from their Babylonian captivity, the rebuilding of the temple in Jerusalem, the people's recommitment to the law as led by Ezra, the rebuilding of the walls of Jerusalem under Nehemiah's leadership, and multiple exhortations to remain faithful to the Lord despite opposition.

To get a fuller picture, it's helpful to look at the books of Ezra and Nehemiah in tandem. Included here is a look at the overlapping people and events, unique features, and unifying themes of the books of Ezra and Nehemiah.

The Book of

Ezra

EZRA WAS A PRIEST
AND SCRIBE.

The Book of

Nehemiah

NEHEMIAH WAS A CUPBEARER TO
THE KING AND LATER BECAME THE
GOVERNOR OF JUDAH.

Themes

Rebuilding

- Foundation of temple
- Altar
- Temple

- Walls of Jerusalem

Opposition

- Opposition to rebuilding the temple
- Construction halted for about fifteen years

- Opposition to rebuilding the walls of Jerusalem
- Continued building while defending against outside threats

Renewal

- The law remembered
- Right worship and practice restored in the temple
- People's renewed commitment to obey

- The law taught to the people
- Renewed commitment to align their lives to God
- Specific vows of obedience

Returns

Zerubbabel

Led a return recorded in the book of Ezra

Ezra

Led a return recorded in the book of Ezra
Ongoing ministry was recorded in both Ezra and Nehemiah

Nehemiah

Led a return recorded in the book of Nehemiah

© 2025 She Reads Truth. All rights reserved.

The Levites *and* Priests

Nehemiah 11:22–36

THE LEVITES AND PRIESTS

²² The leader of the Levites in Jerusalem was Uzzi son of Bani, son of Hashabiah, son of Mattaniah, son of Mica, of the descendants of Asaph, who were singers for the service of God's house. ²³ There was, in fact, a command of the king regarding them, and an ordinance regulating the singers' daily tasks. ²⁴ Pethahiah son of Meshezabel, of the descendants of Zerah son of Judah, was the king's agent in every matter concerning the people.

²⁵ As for the farming settlements with their fields:

Some of Judah's descendants lived in Kiriath-arba
and Dibon and their surrounding villages, and Jekabzeel and its settlements;
²⁶ in Jeshua, Moladah, Beth-pelet,
²⁷ Hazar-shual, and Beer-sheba and its surrounding villages;
²⁸ in Ziklag and Meconah and its surrounding villages;
²⁹ in En-rimmon, Zorah, Jarmuth, and
³⁰ Zanoah and Adullam with their settlements;
in Lachish with its fields and Azekah and its surrounding villages.
So they settled from Beer-sheba to Hinnom Valley.
³¹ Benjamin's descendants:
from Geba, Michmash, Aija,
and Bethel and its surrounding villages,
³² Anathoth, Nob, Ananiah,
³³ Hazor, Ramah, Gittaim,
³⁴ Hadid, Zeboim, Neballat,
³⁵ Lod, and Ono, in Craftsmen's Valley.
³⁶ Some of the Judean divisions of Levites were in Benjamin.

Nehemiah 12:1–26

¹ These are the priests and Levites who went up with Zerubbabel son of Shealtiel and with Jeshua:

Seraiah, Jeremiah, Ezra,
² Amariah, Malluch, Hattush,
³ Shecaniah, Rehum, Meremoth,
⁴ Iddo, Ginnethoi, Abijah,
⁵ Mijamin, Maadiah, Bilgah,
⁶ Shemaiah, Joiarib, Jedaiah,
⁷ Sallu, Amok, Hilkiah, Jedaiah.

These were the heads of the priests and their relatives in the days of Jeshua.

8 The Levites:

Jeshua, Binnui, Kadmiel,
Sherebiah, Judah, and Mattaniah—
he and his relatives were in charge of the songs of praise.
9 Bakbukiah, Unni, and their relatives stood opposite them
in the services.
10 Jeshua fathered Joiakim,
Joiakim fathered Eliashib,
Eliashib fathered Joiada,
11 Joiada fathered Jonathan,
and Jonathan fathered Jaddua.

12 In the days of Joiakim, the heads of the priestly families were

Meraiah	of Seraiah,
Hananiah	of Jeremiah,
13 Meshullam	of Ezra,
Jehohanan	of Amariah,
14 Jonathan	of Malluchi,
Joseph	of Shebaniah,
15 Adna	of Harim,
Helkai	of Meraioth,
16 Zechariah	of Iddo,
Meshullam	of Ginnethon,
17 Zichri	of Abijah,
Piltai	of Moadiah, of Miniamin,
18 Shammua	of Bilgah,
Jehonathan	of Shemaiah,
19 Mattenai	of Joiarib,
Uzzi	of Jedaiah,
20 Kallai	of Sallai,
Eber	of Amok,
21 Hashabiah	of Hilkiah,
and Nethanel	of Jedaiah.

22 In the days of Eliashib, Joiada, Johanan, and Jaddua, the heads of the families of the Levites and priests were recorded while Darius the Persian ruled. 23 Levi's descendants, the family heads, were recorded in the Book of the Historical Events during the days of Johanan son of Eliashib. 24 The heads of the Levites—Hashabiah, Sherebiah, and Jeshua son of Kadmiel, along with their relatives opposite them—gave praise and thanks, division by division, as David the man of God had prescribed. 25 This included Mattaniah, Bakbukiah, and Obadiah. Meshullam, Talmon, and Akkub were gatekeepers who guarded the storerooms at the city gates. 26 These served in the days of Joiakim son of Jeshua, son of Jozadak, and in the days of Nehemiah the governor and Ezra the priest and scribe.

🪶 GOING DEEPER

Numbers 8:13–22

13 "You are to have the Levites stand before Aaron and his sons, and you are to present them before the LORD as a presentation offering. 14 In this way you are to separate the Levites from the rest of the Israelites so that the Levites will belong to me. 15 After that the Levites may come to serve at the tent of meeting, once you have ceremonially cleansed them and presented them as a presentation offering. 16 For they have been exclusively assigned to me from the Israelites. I have taken them for myself in place of all who come first from the womb, every Israelite firstborn. 17 For every firstborn among the Israelites is mine, both man and animal. I consecrated them to myself on the day I struck down every firstborn in the land of Egypt. 18 But I have taken the Levites in place of every firstborn among the Israelites. 19 From the Israelites, I have given the Levites exclusively to Aaron and his sons to perform the work for the Israelites at the tent of meeting and to make atonement on their behalf, so that no plague will come against the Israelites when they approach the sanctuary."

20 Moses, Aaron, and the entire Israelite community did this to the Levites. The Israelites did everything to them the LORD commanded Moses regarding the Levites. 21 The Levites purified themselves and washed their clothes; then Aaron presented them before the LORD as a presentation offering. Aaron also made atonement for them to cleanse them ceremonially. 22 After that, the Levites came to do their work at the tent of meeting in the presence of Aaron and his sons. So they did to them as the LORD had commanded Moses concerning the Levites.

1 Peter 2:9

But you are a chosen race, a royal priesthood, a holy nation, a people for his possession, so that you may proclaim the praises of the one who called you out of darkness into his marvelous light.

Dedication of the Wall

Nehemiah 12:27–47

DEDICATION OF THE WALL

[27] At the dedication of the wall of Jerusalem, they sent for the Levites wherever they lived and brought them to Jerusalem to celebrate the joyous dedication with thanksgiving and singing accompanied by cymbals, harps, and lyres. [28] The singers gathered from the region around Jerusalem, from the settlements of the Netophathites, [29] from Beth-gilgal, and from the fields of Geba and Azmaveth, for they had built settlements for themselves around Jerusalem. [30] After the priests and Levites had purified themselves, they purified the people, the city gates, and the wall.

[31] Then I brought the leaders of Judah up on top of the wall, and I appointed two large processions that gave thanks. One went to the right on the wall, toward the Dung Gate. [32] Hoshaiah and half the leaders of Judah followed, [33] along with Azariah, Ezra, Meshullam, [34] Judah, Benjamin, Shemaiah, Jeremiah, [35] and some of the priests' sons with trumpets, and Zechariah son of Jonathan, son of Shemaiah, son of Mattaniah, son of Micaiah, son of Zaccur, son of Asaph followed [36] as well as his relatives—Shemaiah, Azarel, Milalai, Gilalai, Maai, Nethanel, Judah, and Hanani, with the musical instruments of David, the man of God. Ezra the scribe went in front of them. [37] At the Fountain Gate they climbed the steps of the city of David on the ascent of the wall and went above the house of David to the Water Gate on the east.

[38] The second thanksgiving procession went to the left, and I followed it with half the people along the top of the wall, past the Tower of the Ovens to the Broad Wall, [39] above the Ephraim Gate, and by the Old Gate, the Fish Gate, the Tower of Hananel, and the Tower of the Hundred, to the Sheep Gate. They stopped at the Gate of the Guard. [40] The two thanksgiving processions stood in the house of God. So did I and half of the officials accompanying me, [41] as well as the priests:

Eliakim, Maaseiah, Miniamin,
Micaiah, Elioenai, Zechariah,
and Hananiah, with trumpets;
[42] and Maaseiah, Shemaiah, Eleazar,
Uzzi, Jehohanan, Malchijah, Elam, and Ezer.

Then the singers sang, with Jezrahiah as the leader. [43] On that day they offered great sacrifices and rejoiced because God had given them great joy. The women and children also celebrated, and Jerusalem's rejoicing was heard far away.

SUPPORT OF THE LEVITES' MINISTRY

[44] On that same day men were placed in charge of the rooms that housed the supplies, contributions, firstfruits, and tenths. The legally required portions for the

priests and Levites were gathered from the village fields, because Judah was grateful to the priests and Levites who were serving. [45] They performed the service of their God and the service of purification, along with the singers and gatekeepers, as David and his son Solomon had prescribed. [46] For long ago, in the days of David and Asaph, there were heads of the singers and songs of praise and thanksgiving to God. [47] So in the days of Zerubbabel and Nehemiah, all Israel contributed the daily portions for the singers and gatekeepers. They also set aside daily portions for the Levites, and the Levites set aside daily portions for Aaron's descendants.

◗ GOING DEEPER

Isaiah 62:1–7
ZION'S RESTORATION

[1] I will not keep silent because of Zion,
and I will not keep still because of Jerusalem,
until her righteousness shines like a bright light
and her salvation, like a flaming torch.

[2] Nations will see your righteousness
and all kings, your glory.
You will be given a new name
that the LORD's mouth will announce.

[3] You will be a glorious crown in the LORD's hand,
and a royal diadem in the palm of your God's hand.
[4] You will no longer be called Deserted,
and your land will not be called Desolate;
instead, you will be called My Delight Is in Her,
and your land Married;
for the LORD delights in you,
and your land will be married.
[5] For as a young man marries a young woman,
so your sons will marry you;
and as a groom rejoices over his bride,
so your God will rejoice over you.
[6] Jerusalem,
I have appointed watchmen on your walls;
they will never be silent, day or night.
There is no rest for you,
who remind the LORD.
[7] Do not give him rest
until he establishes and makes Jerusalem
the praise of the earth.

The Walls

of

Jerusalem

in Jesus's Time

The centerpiece of the Christian faith—the death and resurrection of Jesus—took place in Jerusalem just a few hundred years after the time of Nehemiah. During that time, the city grew and its walls were expanded. This map displays Jerusalem and its walls during the ministry of Jesus, along with a few corresponding events in Jesus's ministry that happened in and around Jerusalem. Turn back to the first map on page 50 to see how the city developed over time.

A   Jesus was dedicated as a child in the temple.
Lk 2:21–24

Jesus displayed understanding and wisdom as a twelve year old among teachers in the temple.
Lk 2:41–50

Jesus cleansed the temple.
Lk 19:45–47

Jesus healed in the temple.
Mt 21:14–16

B   Jesus sent the man born blind to the pool of Siloam.
Jn 9:1–7

C   Jesus shared the Passover meal with His disciples.
Lk 22:8–20

D   Jesus prayed and was arrested in the garden of Gesthemane.
Mt 26:36–50

E   Jesus appeared before Pilate in Herod's fortress.
Mt 27:1–2, 11–26

F   Jesus was crucified at Golgotha.
Jn 19:16–17

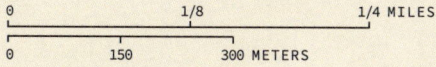

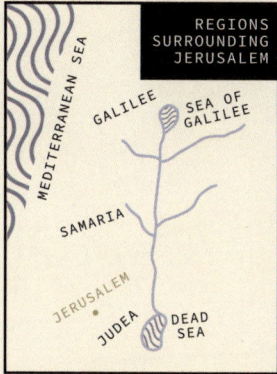

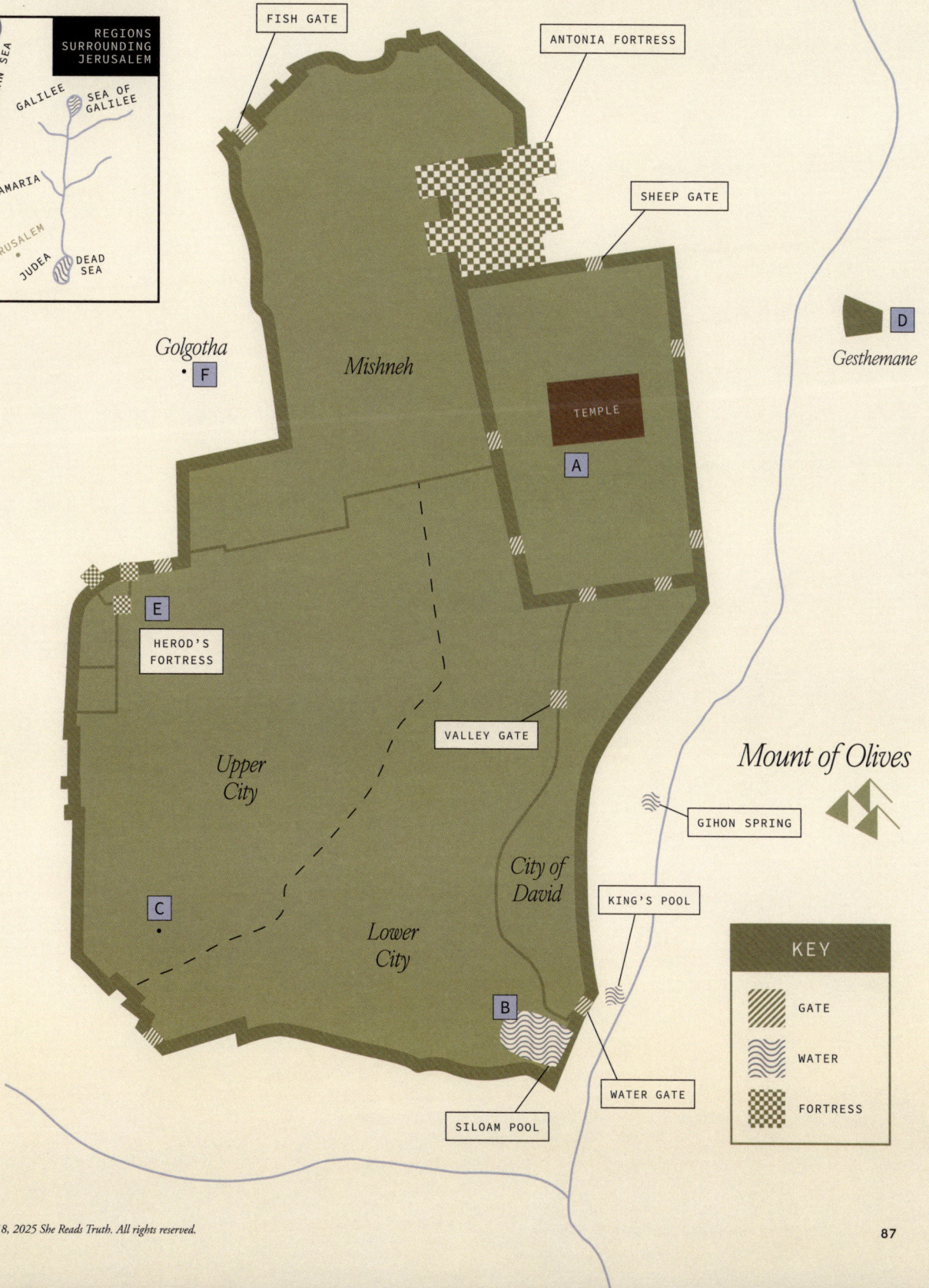

Scale

0 — 1/8 — 1/4 MILES

0 — 150 — 300 METERS

REGIONS SURROUNDING JERUSALEM

MEDITERRANEAN SEA

GALILEE

SEA OF GALILEE

SAMARIA

JERUSALEM

JUDEA

DEAD SEA

FISH GATE

ANTONIA FORTRESS

SHEEP GATE

Golgotha

F

Mishneh

Gesthemane

D

TEMPLE

A

E

HEROD'S FORTRESS

Upper City

VALLEY GATE

Mount of Olives

GIHON SPRING

C

City of David

KING'S POOL

Lower City

B

Water Gate

SILOAM POOL

KEY

GATE

WATER

FORTRESS

© 2018, 2025 She Reads Truth. All rights reserved.

REMEMBER ME FOR THIS, MY GOD, AND DON'T ERASE THE
DEEDS OF FAITHFUL LOVE I HAVE DONE FOR THE HOUSE
OF MY GOD AND FOR ITS SERVICES.

Nehemiah 13:14

Further Reforms

Nehemiah 13

NEHEMIAH'S FURTHER REFORMS

[1] At that time the book of Moses was read publicly to the people. The command was found written in it that no Ammonite or Moabite should ever enter the assembly of God, [2] because they did not meet the Israelites with food and water. Instead, they hired Balaam against them to curse them, but our God turned the curse into a blessing. [3] When they heard the law, they separated all those of mixed descent from Israel.

[4] Now before this, the priest Eliashib had been put in charge of the storerooms of the house of our God. He was a relative of Tobiah [5] and had prepared a large room for him where they had previously stored the grain offerings, the frankincense, the articles, and the tenths of grain, new wine, and fresh oil prescribed for the Levites, singers, and gatekeepers, along with the contributions for the priests.

[6] While all this was happening, I was not in Jerusalem, because I had returned to King Artaxerxes of Babylon in the thirty-second year of his reign. It was only later that I asked the king for a leave of absence [7] so I could return to Jerusalem. Then I discovered the evil that Eliashib had done on behalf of Tobiah by providing him a room in the courts of God's house. [8] I was greatly displeased and threw all of Tobiah's household possessions out of the room. [9] I ordered that the rooms be purified, and I had the articles of the house of God restored there, along with the grain offering and frankincense. [10] I also found out that because the portions for the Levites had not been given, each of the Levites and the singers performing the service had gone back to his own field. [11] Therefore, I rebuked the officials, asking, "Why has the house of God been neglected?" I gathered the Levites and singers together and stationed them at their posts. [12] Then all Judah brought a tenth of the grain, new wine, and fresh oil into the storehouses. [13] I appointed as treasurers over the storehouses the priest Shelemiah, the scribe Zadok, and Pedaiah of the Levites, with Hanan son of Zaccur, son of Mattaniah to assist them, because they were considered trustworthy. They were responsible for the distribution to their colleagues.

[14] Remember me for this, my God, and don't erase the deeds of faithful love I have done for the house of my God and for its services.

[15] At that time I saw people in Judah treading winepresses on the Sabbath. They were also bringing in stores of grain and loading them on donkeys, along with wine, grapes, and figs. All kinds of goods were being brought to Jerusalem on the Sabbath day. So I warned them against selling food on that day. [16] The Tyrians living there were importing fish and all kinds of merchandise and selling them on the Sabbath to the people of Judah in Jerusalem.

[17] I rebuked the nobles of Judah and said to them, "What is this evil you are doing—profaning the Sabbath day?

¹⁸ Didn't your ancestors do the same, so that our God brought all this disaster on us and on this city? And now you are rekindling his anger against Israel by profaning the Sabbath!"

¹⁹ When shadows began to fall on the city gates of Jerusalem just before the Sabbath, I gave orders that the city gates be closed and not opened until after the Sabbath. I posted some of my men at the gates, so that no goods could enter during the Sabbath day. ²⁰ Once or twice the merchants and those who sell all kinds of goods camped outside Jerusalem, ²¹ but I warned them, "Why are you camping in front of the wall? If you do it again, I'll use force against you." After that they did not come again on the Sabbath. ²² Then I instructed the Levites to purify themselves and guard the city gates in order to keep the Sabbath day holy.

Remember me for this also, my God, and look on me with compassion according to the abundance of your faithful love.

²³ In those days I also saw Jews who had married women from Ashdod, Ammon, and Moab. ²⁴ Half of their children spoke the language of Ashdod or the language of one of the other peoples but could not speak Hebrew. ²⁵ I rebuked them, cursed them, beat some of their men, and pulled out their hair. I forced them to take an oath before God and said, "You must not give your daughters in marriage to their sons or take their daughters as wives for your sons or yourselves! ²⁶ Didn't King Solomon of Israel sin in matters like this? There was not a king like him among many nations. He was loved by his God, and God made him king over all Israel, yet foreign women drew him into sin. ²⁷ Why then should we hear about you doing all this terrible evil and acting unfaithfully against our God by marrying foreign women?" ²⁸ Even one of the sons of Jehoiada, son of the high priest Eliashib, had become a son-in-law to Sanballat the Horonite. So I drove him away from me.

²⁹ Remember them, my God, for defiling the priesthood as well as the covenant of the priesthood and the Levites.

³⁰ So I purified them from everything foreign and assigned specific duties to each of the priests and Levites. ³¹ I also arranged for the donation of wood at the appointed times and for the firstfruits.

Remember me, my God, with favor.

Though the returned exiles had recommitted their lives to the whole of God's law (Neh 9:38; 10:29), Nehemiah 10:30-39 (which you read about on Day 15) includes specific vows the people made to follow God's commands concerning marriage, the Sabbath, the temple tax, and offerings. Nehemiah's reforms listed here address each of these commands, demonstrating how, over time, the nation had strayed from their commitment to God.

♥ GOING DEEPER

Psalm 25:6–7

[6] Remember, LORD, your compassion
and your faithful love,
for they have existed from antiquity.
[7] Do not remember the sins of my youth
or my acts of rebellion;
in keeping with your faithful love, remember me
because of your goodness, LORD.

Hebrews 3:12–14

[12] Watch out, brothers and sisters, so that there won't be in any of you an evil, unbelieving heart that turns away from the living God. [13] But encourage each other daily, while it is still called today, so that none of you is hardened by sin's deception. [14] For we have become participants in Christ if we hold firmly until the end the reality that we had at the start.

Week 3
Response

Use the following questions to reflect on how the themes of
repentance and renewal *are at work in the book of Nehemiah.*

01   Why did God's people need to repent?

02   How was God's law used to renew the identity of His people?

03   How are God's commands shaping your everyday life?

Grace Day

TAKE THIS DAY TO CATCH UP ON YOUR
READING, PRAY, AND REST IN THE
PRESENCE OF THE LORD.

At that time I will bring
you back, yes, at *the* time
I will gather you. I will
give you fame *and* praise
among all *the* peoples of
the earth, when I restore
your fortunes before
your eyes. *The* LORD
has spoken.

Zephaniah 3:20

Weekly Truth

SCRIPTURE IS GOD BREATHED AND TRUE.
WHEN WE MEMORIZE IT, WE CARRY HIS
WORD WITH US WHEREVER WE GO.

THROUGHOUT THIS PLAN, WE HAVE
BEEN MEMORIZING NEHEMIAH 13:22B, A
REMINDER OF GOD'S HEART TOWARD US
AS WE SEEK TO OBEY HIM. THIS WEEK,
COMMIT THE ENTIRETY OF IT TO MEMORY.

SEE TIPS FOR MEMORIZING
SCRIPTURE ON PAGE 100.

Remember me for this also,
my God, and look on me
with compassion according
to the abundance of your
faithful love.

Nehemiah 13:22b

BENEDICTION

Go around Zion, encircle it;
count its towers, note its ramparts;
tour its citadels so that you can
tell *a* future generation: "This God,
our God forever *and* ever—he will
always lead us."

Psalm 48:11–12

Tips for Memorizing Scripture

At She Reads Truth, we believe Scripture memorization is an important discipline in your walk with God. Committing God's Word to memory means we carry it with us and we can minister to others wherever we go. As you approach the Weekly Truth verse in this book, try these memorization tips to see which techniques work best for you!

STUDY IT

Study the passage in its biblical context, and ask yourself a few questions before you begin to memorize it: What does this passage say? What does it mean? How would I say this in my own words? What does it teach me about God? Understanding what the passage means helps you know why it is important to carry it with you wherever you go.

Break the passage into smaller sections, memorizing a phrase at a time.

PRAY IT

Use the passage you are memorizing as a prompt for prayer.

WRITE IT

Dedicate a notebook to Scripture memorization, and write the passage over and over again.

Diagram the passage after you write it out. Place a square around the verbs, underline the nouns, and circle any adjectives or adverbs. Say the passage aloud several times, emphasizing the verbs as you repeat it. Then do the same thing again with the nouns, then the adjectives and adverbs.

Write out the first letter of each word in the passage somewhere you can reference it throughout the week as you work on your memorization.

Use a whiteboard to write out the passage. Erase a few words at a time as you continue to repeat it aloud. Keep erasing parts of the passage until you have it all committed to memory.

CREATE

If you can, make up a tune for the passage to sing as you go about your day, or try singing it to the tune of a favorite song.

Sketch the passage, visualizing what each phrase would look like in the form of a picture. Or try using calligraphy or altering the style of your handwriting as you write it out.

Use hand signals or signs to come up with associations for each word or phrase and repeat the movements as you practice.

SAY IT

Repeat the passage out loud to yourself as you are going through the rhythm of your day—getting ready, pouring your coffee, waiting in traffic, or making dinner.

Listen to the passage read aloud to you.

Record a voice memo on your phone, and listen to it throughout the day or play it on an audio Bible.

SHARE IT

Memorize the passage with a friend, family member, or mentor. Spontaneously challenge each other to recite the passage, or pick a time to review your passage and practice saying it from memory together.

Send the passage as an encouraging text to a friend, testing yourself as you type to see how much you have memorized so far.

KEEP AT IT!

Set reminders on your phone to prompt you to practice your passage.

Purchase a She Reads Truth Scripture Card Set, or keep a stack of note cards with Scripture you are memorizing by your bed. Practice reciting what you've memorized previously before you go to sleep, ending with the passages you are currently learning. If you wake up in the middle of the night, review them again instead of grabbing your phone. Read them out loud before you get out of bed in the morning.

© 2021 She Reads Truth. All rights reserved.

CSB BOOK ABBREVIATIONS

OLD TESTAMENT

GN Genesis	**JB** Job	**HAB** Habakkuk	**PHP** Philippians
EX Exodus	**PS** Psalms	**ZPH** Zephaniah	**COL** Colossians
LV Leviticus	**PR** Proverbs	**HG** Haggai	**1TH** 1 Thessalonians
NM Numbers	**EC** Ecclesiastes	**ZCH** Zechariah	**2TH** 2 Thessalonians
DT Deuteronomy	**SG** Song of Solomon	**MAL** Malachi	**1TM** 1 Timothy
JOS Joshua	**IS** Isaiah		**2TM** 2 Timothy
JDG Judges	**JR** Jeremiah		**TI** Titus
RU Ruth	**LM** Lamentations	**NEW TESTAMENT**	**PHM** Philemon
1SM 1 Samuel	**EZK** Ezekiel	**MT** Matthew	**HEB** Hebrews
2SM 2 Samuel	**DN** Daniel	**MK** Mark	**JMS** James
1KG 1 Kings	**HS** Hosea	**LK** Luke	**1PT** 1 Peter
2KG 2 Kings	**JL** Joel	**JN** John	**2PT** 2 Peter
1CH 1 Chronicles	**AM** Amos	**AC** Acts	**1JN** 1 John
2CH 2 Chronicles	**OB** Obadiah	**RM** Romans	**2JN** 2 John
EZR Ezra	**JNH** Jonah	**1CO** 1 Corinthians	**3JN** 3 John
NEH Nehemiah	**MC** Micah	**2CO** 2 Corinthians	**JD** Jude
EST Esther	**NAH** Nahum	**GL** Galatians	**RV** Revelation
		EPH Ephesians	

BIBLIOGRAPHY

Bilkes, Gerald M. "Ahasuerus." In *Eerdmans Dictionary of the Bible,* edited by David Noel Freedman, Allen C. Myers, and Astrid B. Beck. Eerdmans, 2000.

Bilkes, Gerald M. "Artaxerxes." In *Eerdmans Dictionary of the Bible,* edited by David Noel Freedman, Allen C. Myers, and Astrid B. Beck. Eerdmans, 2000.

Logos Bible Software. *Jerusalem in the Times of Ezra and Nehemiah.* 2007.

Logos Bible Software. *New Testament Jerusalem.* 2007.

Mackie, Tim. "Tim Mackie: Ezra-Nehemiah Training." Seattle Area Pastors Network. August 2017. 4 hrs., 25 min., 16 sec. https://vimeo.com/211179978.

"Post-Exilic Jerusalem ca. 440 b.c." In *The Carta Bible Atlas,* edited by Yohanan Aharoni, Anson F. Rainey, Michael Avi-Yonah, Ze'ev Safrai, and R. Steven Notley. 5th ed. The Israel Map and Publishing Company, Ltd., 2011.

You just spent 21 days in the Word of God!

**MY FAVORITE DAY OF
THIS READING PLAN:**

**ONE THING I LEARNED
ABOUT GOD:**

**WHAT WAS GOD DOING IN
MY LIFE DURING THIS STUDY?**

HOW DID I FIND DELIGHT IN GOD'S WORD?

**WHAT DID I LEARN THAT I WANT TO SHARE
WITH SOMEONE ELSE?**

**A SPECIFIC PASSAGE OR VERSE
THAT ENCOURAGED ME:**

**A SPECIFIC PASSAGE OR VERSE THAT
CHALLENGED AND CONVICTED ME:**